# LETTERS OF ÉTIENNE GILSON
## TO HENRI DE LUBAC

# LETTERS OF ÉTIENNE GILSON TO HENRI DE LUBAC

Annotated by Father de Lubac

Translated by Mary Emily Hamilton

IGNATIUS PRESS    SAN FRANCISCO

Title of the French original:
*Lettres de M. Étienne Gilson*
*adressées au P. Henri de Lubac*
*et commentées par celui-ci*
© 1986 Les Éditions du Cerf
Paris

Cover art by Keith W. Criss
Cover design and calligraphy by Victoria Hoke Lane

© 1988 Ignatius Press, San Francisco
All rights reserved
ISBN 0-89870-184-8
Library of Congress Catalogue Number 87-82565
Printed in the United States of America

# CONTENTS

# FOREWORD

I have found, here and there, nineteen letters received from M. Étienne Gilson. (There might have been more that got lost in the course of moving or culling files in too great a hurry.) Several of them are short; none of them is without interest, if one wants to learn something about their author's personality, his doctrinal positions, or the various internal conflicts that have beset the Church in our day. They go from July 8, 1956, to July 1, 1975; the last one is written in someone else's handwriting. (I did not save any copies of my own letters to M. Gilson.)

We got to know each other rather late in life. Spending my adolescence in the provinces, with the war years intervening between youth and the prolonged classical education one needs in order to be a Jesuit (all of which I received outside of France), followed immediately by a newly created, very busy teaching assignment in the theology department at Lyon—all these things kept me away from the academic atmosphere and the groups of Thomists in the capital. However, during my philosophy studies on Jersey, I had read Étienne Gilson's fundamental book on Saint

Thomas Aquinas (in its second edition, published by Vrin, 1922).[1] It was on the shelf, under the category marked "Modern Philosophy", in the bookcase of light reading that was generously unlocked for us during holidays. What a happy time that was, when each one of these little privileges meant so much![2] I used to like to balance this book with Rousselot's thesis on Saint Thomas' intellectualism—a very different thesis, which I discovered with delight at Canterbury in the early months of 1920, and one that (as I learned later) M. Gilson himself very much admired.[3] Then, when I got to Paris, I went once or twice to hear the professor at the Sorbonne speak on Saint Bernard; and later, when he was teaching at the Collège de France, on "l'Être et l'Essence", but I stayed in the safe anonymity of the audience—although people told me later on that he had spotted me right away in the crowd.

Only at the beginning of the fifties, when I was staying in Paris for a short while, did we really have a chance to become friends. Our first meetings, if I remember correctly, took place under the auspices of Joseph Vrin, in his pleasant publishing house. They were rather brief and unemotional—yet there was immediately a respectful but strong friendship. Notwithstanding the rarity of our meetings, our friendship never ceased to grow. For him, the friendship was mingled with an indulgent quality of understanding and an

8

almost paternal kindliness; for me, with a kind of respectful wonder and a feeling of gratitude for a haven of peace where, when things got rough, I could rely on his trust.

I have a number of lively memories that are very dear to recall. There was a time when he was in the habit of coming to the Institute's library on Monday afternoons. I used to meet him there after the Academy of Moral Sciences' meeting. He always had a good story to tell me—sometimes more than one—that caused him several times to pop out of his carrel directly opposite my own, like a Jack-in-the-box, his face lit up with a mischievous grin. One evening, lingering to talk a little longer, half-jokingly, half-seriously, he explained to me how he had led his working life backwards, finding himself forced at every stage to go back through history to understand, always too late, the point of the study he had already completed. He had finally arrived, he told me, at the huge field of patristics, on which he ought to have started to work a long time before. . . . But this was a very much oversimplified view of what he really did, since in order to understand Descartes better, he had first explored the Scholastics from generation to generation,[4] going back and forth from them to Descartes more than once. Later, he worked in several fields at once and, as early as 1929, produced his fine *Introduction à l'étude de saint Augustin*.[5]

While the Sorbonne was solemnly celebrating the hundredth anniversary of Bergson's birth—this was in May 1959, at the Tenth Congress of French-Speaking Philosophical Societies—an incident occurred during the May 18 meeting dedicated to religion, in the Richelieu Auditorium, which M. Henri Gouhier has recently recounted.[6] Among the papers that had been submitted, there was one by Father Joseph de Tonquédec—a philosopher and a rigorous theologian, aged eighty—on "la conception bergsonienne de Dieu" [Bergson's concept of God] that was a bit of a diatribe. After the reader, Georges Le Roy, had presented the paper, its author interjected some of his own comments, rather bitter in tone, into the discussion that followed. The president, Monsignor de Rayemaeker (from Louvain), was about to call a recess when Gilson, who up to then had been having trouble keeping quiet, jumped up, and thinking on his feet, and lightning fast, took up his teacher's defense.[7] Something else happened, however, that does not come into M. Gouhier's account. A few moments later, in the courtyard where everyone had gone for a breath of air, a little knot of people gathered around Gilson, who was still not pacified. On the contrary, he was more fired up than ever. In front of an audience that was growing larger and larger, drawn at first by curiosity, then spellbound, he began again his hymn of gratitude to Bergson. In order better to glorify the liberating work of Bergson, he held up in stark contrast, with a freedom he wouldn't have allowed himself in the formal meeting, a certain kind of Scholasticism that was fashionable at the time. While doing justice to the few eternal verities this Scholasticism was still able to convey, he criticized, in a comic way that mitigated his diagnostic severity, its out-of-date methods, its lack of historical sense, the ignorance of or the snobbish inability to understand the latest research, the need to create heretics to cut up—in short, he criticized a spirit that was taking shape in systems which were becoming more rigid the more unfaithful they were to tradition, a spirit quite other than the Angelic Doctor's. He spoke almost in a kind of code, he mentioned no names and his final conclusions were still veiled; but the knowing looks he shot at me, at a time when we understood each other very well, left me in no doubt: as he did in a number of his letters, Étienne Gilson wanted to encourage me again to *stand firm* in the spiritual combat in which I found myself engaged.

Obviously, Gilson had no fear of making clear-cut judgments. For example, he did not like Blondel; he pushed aside his method of problem-solving, and, not daring to condemn him, made as if he did not understand him. While he paid his respects to Father Teilhard de Chardin as a religious, he hated his work as a whole, even though he was not familiar with it. (He was just as unfair to Blondel as he was to Teilhard.) But he nevertheless grasped how much I was attached to them, for various reasons, and that never cast a shadow over his friendship toward me. Even though his quest for the truth seldom strayed from the furrows his plough had traced, his heart remained generous and as big as all outdoors. Besides our mutual sympathy and our common basic understanding of doctrinal and historical points that were then being bitterly argued, we both had a certain taste for humanism (but how poor mine was, compared with his!). Then, too, I think I can say we had an unspoken secret: early on, he guessed that I felt compassion for his sufferings, indeed part of them were the same for us both. Without exchanging confidences, we were still bound by a firm bond of true friendship.

After we met in Paris, we found ourselves in Rome in September 1965, before the Council had ended, for a Thomist Congress that, although it did not clash with his ideas as violently as the one in 1950, clearly held no excitement for him. Then there was, in 1967, the Toronto Theological Congress,[8] where we were both speakers. At the same time, in the city, they were celebrating the centennial of the Canadian Confederation. All the Canadian Catholic bishops were there; the Pope had sent a legate. At the Solemn Mass of Thanksgiving, Étienne Gilson read the Epistle, in French:

it was the hymn to Christ from the Epistle to the Ephesians. After the Mass, on the raised square in front of the cathedral, in the midst of the crowd, he waxed lyrical as he glorified the unsurpassable beauty of the Catholic High Mass; and then, radiant with joy, he gave me a huge bear-hug.

You could tell he felt at home in Toronto, at the Pontifical Institute of Mediaeval Studies that he had helped to found in 1929, where he had completed numerous, more or less prolonged teaching assignments, and where he was loved.[9] When he was there, he felt young again. There were further special occasions when he had the same feeling. Such was the case in December 1968 at the Institut catholique in Paris—the last time, I think, that I saw him. They were celebrating another hundredth anniversary, the centennial of the birth of Claudel, that impetuous genius whom we both admired, and who was all the dearer to us now that it had become stylish, even among the clergy, to cast aspersions on him. I was scheduled to give a brief talk, serving as a sort of curtain-raiser to Étienne Gilson's lecture on "Claudel poète catholique". No subject could have suited him better. Claudel was for him what Virgil was for Claudel: the Poet par excellence. His name, he told us right off the bat, "is one of those that make my heart beat faster". (Doubtless, too, in his modesty, he recognized a certain kinship with this "knight mounted on a skittish horse, who can neither get used to the horse nor dismount".) Laying out his magnificent fresco before us, he was in his element. Quoting Claudel's poems, he acted them out with his voice and gestures. Never was he more sparkling, more radiant, more dazzling—more youthful.[10]

. . . Yet the dark years were already coming on. To the increasing pains of old age were added the increasing pain that this son of the Church— this faithful and far-seeing Catholic—felt due to the feverish rot that was eating away at the seamless robe from every side. Those who aggravated this fever fraudulently claimed the recent Council's authority. Many people let themselves get caught up in this. Others became tense, trying to keep out of it and not quite knowing how. The venerable philosopher's tentative efforts to offer a remedy for the crisis seemed to him, right to the end of his life, to have been all in vain. Even the grand letter of recognition Paul VI sent him in 1975, right after his ninetieth birthday, hardly found any echo in France.

How I wish that in those days I could have thrown to the winds the discretion that had always, by tacit agreement, characterized our relationship, so that I could have done more to comfort him! For his part, although he had reached the limit of his strength and was bedridden, he tried one last time, in his very last message, to let me know once again how faithful a friend he was. That was the first of July, 1975.

H.L.

The years have passed, times have changed, and I don't think there is any danger now of my being indiscreet if I publish these letters uncut, giving in the annotations the suitable explanations.

[1] In 1913–1914, Gilson had given a public lecture series at Lille on "le système de Thomas d'Aquin". It was not yet time for this to have been a result of a particular attachment to Thomism, but he did have a deliberate wish to reintroduce the history of medieval thought into the university curriculum. (In 1922, at Strasbourg, he published *La Philosophie au Moyen Age*; it enjoyed lasting success and grew to be a thick volume in 1944.) With that, he broke with Cousin's interpretation of history, which held that there had been "but two distinguishable eras in the history of philosophy, as there had been but two in the history of the world: the ancient and the modern era"; between these two ages, the light of Greek genius "gradually dimmed in the night of the Middle Ages . . . , the modern era began with Descartes" (Cousin, "Cours de philosophie de 1818", cited in É. Gilson, *Le Philosophe et la théologie* [Fayard, 1960], 97–98). Contrary to Gilson's first fears, the rector of the University of Lyon favored and welcomed this initiative—but not one single clergyman took the course. Fortunat Strowski was going to publish it in his *Revue des cours et conférences,* but the

war, in August 1916, interrupted the publication. Having revised and completed his text, Gilson had *Le Thomisme, introduction au système de saint Thomas d'Aquin* published at Strasbourg in 1919. "This book", he would write in 1960, "was to stand as a monument erected by its own author to his own ignorance of the questions of which he spoke" (ibid., 102). The second edition (Paris, 1922), less dependent on modern Thomists, contained a more penetrating analysis of the actual text of Saint Thomas. The third edition was dated 1927, the fifth, 1945; the sixth and last, 1965. Each one brought in something new. Cf. Laurence K. Shook, *Étienne Gilson,* The Étienne Gilson Series, 6 (New York: Pontifical Institute of Mediaeval Studies, 1984, hereafter cited as *Gilson*), 61–62, 96, 111–112.

[2]Two years later, at Hastings, his *Philosophie de saint Bonaventure* was less hospitably received by our teachers. For some time, the work was excluded as dangerous from the undergraduates' theological library. It is true, there was a professor who wasn't quite so strict, to whom we could go to borrow it. As early as 1913, at Lille, Gilson planned a course on Bonaventure; in October 1914, he was reading him in the La Courtine Army Camp; while he was a prisoner in Germany, he studied the *De humanae cognitionis ratione,* a collection of writings by Bonaventure and his disciples published at Quaracchi in 1883. Starting in 1921, at the École Pratique des Hautes-Études of the University of Paris, he continued his research into Bonaventure and the Franciscan tradition.

[3]"Pierre Rousselot, S.J., the first to announce the renewal of interest in the Thomism of Saint Thomas that would free us from so many uncertainties, killed at the front [in World War I], buried in the mud of the Les Éparges battlefield . . ." (Gilson, *Philosophe et théologie,* 58–59). Between 1910 and 1913, Gilson had met Rousselot briefly when Rousselot was a young professor at the Institut catholique de Paris and

secretary of the journal *Recherches de science religieuse* that had just been founded by Fathers Grandmaison and Lebreton, a journal inaugurated with his two articles on "les yeux de la foi" [the eyes of faith] that were immediately famous and also immediately provoked bitter controversy. Gilson is alluding here to his Sorbonne thesis: *L'Intellectualisme de saint Thomas* (Alcan, 1908). (The objections I could not help raising to it did not take anything away from my admiration of Rousselot's thesis.)

[4] Gilson did not succeed all at once in determining Descartes' historical situation in relation to early Scholasticism. See on this subject the succession of his writings from 1913 to 1948. Cf. Jean-Luc Marion, "L'instauration de la rupture: Gilson à la lecture de Descartes", in *Étienne Gilson et nous* (Vrin, 1960), 13–34. In the *Bulletin thomiste*, July 1929, speaking of Gilson, Father Simonin, one of the most perceptive of the Thomists, observed that "thirteenth-century Scholasticism is not endowed, in the same way as sixteenth-century Scholasticism is, with a well-defined form of Scholastic thought, of the kind that was most influential from that time on, that was called Suarezianism."

[5] Prepared as early as 1921 by his work at the École Pratique des Hautes Études on "l'illumination divine dans Augustin" and "l'influence d'Augustin et le rôle de la foi dans la philosophie médiévale". ("This work, more than sixty-five years old, has not been superseded; it remains definitive" [G. Madec, in *Revue des études augustiniennes*, 1984: 366].) Gilson will begin his courses at the Collège de France, in December 1945, dealing with "la dialectique de l'être et de l'existence chez saint Augustin"; from then on he constantly goes back to the study of the *Confessions*, "that inexhaustible book". In 1961, he gave a seminar at the Toronto Institute on books 11 and 12 of the *Confessions*.

[6] A student and ever-faithful friend of Gilson's, he succeeded him in the Académie française in 1979, and was

happy to be able to give a eulogy of Gilson on that occasion.

[7] "When I go back to 1905–1908, and as I hear how he is criticized today by a number of theologians . . . , I feel very much surprised. Really, who was it that brought metaphysics back to us when everybody said metaphysics was dead? It was Bergson. Who taught us how to express, in a new way, in precise, intelligible terms, problems like those of liberty, the nature of the soul, its immortality, the origin and the nature of the universe? It was Bergson. . . . What we have later become, sometimes in ways very different from his own, we have become thanks to him. . . . If many of us have kept our Faith, or if we have found it again, we do not owe that to the manuals of neo-Scholastic philosophy. . . . Quite simply, that is what I wanted to thank him for" (in *Bergson et nous*, Proceedings of the Tenth Congress of French-Speaking Philosophical Societies [Actes du X$^e$ congrès des Sociétés de philosophie de langue française], Paris, May 17–19, 1959, pp. 277–278, cited by H. Gouhier, in his speech on his reception into the Académie française, November 22, 1979). Cf. Gilson's speech when he was received into the Académie (1946): Bergson had made him see that, even after Kant's critiques and Comte's positivism, metaphysical knowledge was still possible. As early as 1941, in *God and Philosophy*, 2nd ed. (Yale University Press, 1960), page xii: ". . . Bergson, the genius whose lectures still remain in my memory as so many hours of intellectual transfiguration. . . ." In 1960, he recalled the "case of Bergson" at length in *Le Philosophe et la théologie,* chapters 6, 7, and 8, pp. 121–189: "What we came looking for at the Sorbonne, and what she refused us, . . . the Collège de France gave us in profusion. . . . What does Bergson not have a right to, in the way of gratitude, from the young friends of metaphysics whom he found wandering in the wilderness of scientism, and brought them forth!" (p. 134; cf. 150).

[8]Cf. L. K. Shook, *Gilson*. Gilson took one last trip to Toronto in 1971; he was eighty-seven years old. He had three close friends there, who were successively directors of the Institute: Father Gerald Phelan, Anton G. Pegis, and Father Laurence K. Shook. One day Gilson said of Phelan: "Strong faith, keen intelligence, broad culture, training in languages and music" (Shook, *Gilson*, 187); in 1935, he dedicated his book *Le Réalisme méthodique* "to my Friend the Rev. Dr. G. B. Phelan, Director of the Institute of Mediaeval Studies. . . ." In 1957, Pegis published in New York *A Gilson Reader: Writings of Étienne Gilson*, edited with an introduction by Anton G. Pegis.

[9]On November 3, 1944, after a long, silent separation because of the war and the German occupation, he wrote to Phelan: "What a joy to write to you again! I can hardly believe it is true. . . . As for myself, I have been teaching, writing and praying, without ever forgetting to pray for you, for the Institute and for all friends. Toronto was in my memory as an earthly paradise, full of good friends, and good things . . ." (Shook, *Gilson*, 250–251).

[10]Text in *Nouvelles de l'Institut catholique de Paris*, no. 1 (January 1969). It would be interesting to compare it with the "Petit mémoire sur Paul Claudel", by Hans Urs von Balthasar, which is on the same subject: *Bulletin de la Société Paul Claudel* 81 (First Quarter 1981).

# LETTERS
## 1956–1975

6, rue Collet, Vermenton, Yonne

July 8, 1956

Reverend and dear Father,

I have just read the third edition of *Sur les chemins de Dieu*[1] with so much pleasure that I can't keep from writing to tell you. The theological anthropomorphism you are concerned about seems to me to be one of the main obstacles to belief in God, especially among intellectuals. Father Sertillanges, whom you so appropriately cite, fought it with all his strength.[2] Unfortunately, theological anthropomorphism has patronage in very high places, and this is precisely why it is such a large-scale, ongoing project to straighten out people's understanding of Saint Thomas Aquinas. People conjure up a Thomism after the manner of the Schools, a sort of dull rationalism which panders to the kind of deism that most of them, deep down, really prefer to teach.[3]

Our only salvation lies in a return to Saint Thomas himself, before the Thomism of John of

Saint Thomas, before that of Cajetan as well—
Cajetan, whose famous commentary is in every
respect the consummate example of a *corruptorium
Thomae*.[4]

God is QUI EST; in God, that which in other
beings is their essence, is God's act of existing,
the EST. Now, in the proposition *Deus est*, we
know that what the proposition says is true,
but we don't know what the verb *est* means. I
don't remember whether you cited the decisive
text of the *Summa Theologiae* I, 3, 4, ad 2. Neither Father Sertillanges, nor you yourself, nor
anybody will ever get any further by calling
into question what Saint Thomas, over-boldly
but correctly, named an "agnosticism of depic-
tion".[5]

Yet, in order to have the right to go even this
far, one must face up to the Thomist metaphysic
of the *esse*. The theologians fully understand this
point because, even in the Order of Friars
Preachers, from Hervé Nedellec right on up to
Cajetan and beyond, so many of them have taken
such great pains to camouflage the authentic teaching of the master.[6] Let us say, rather, to emasculate
his doctrine and to make of his theology a brew
of watered-down *philosophia aristotelico-thomistica*
concocted to give off a vague deism fit only for
the use of right-thinking candidates for high-
school diplomas and Arts degrees. Salvation lies
in returning to the real Saint Thomas,[7] rightly

called the Universal Doctor of the Church; accept no substitutes!

Please know, reverend and dear Father, how much I appreciate your sending your book. Why not consider doing with other books, where your thinking was correct without your having found your language perfectly precise,[8] what you have just done with this one? Who has ever denied that, *de potentia Dei absoluta*, God could have created man without the possibility for everlasting blessedness? Nobody! But from the viewpoint of the final cause, which is the highest of causes, every evidence, both in the world *and in mankind as God created them*, points to the supernatural end for which God destined us. In short, according to the *Contra Gentiles*, the structure and nature of created man are those of a being called to eternal bliss.[9] But who cares, these days, about the final cause? It's only the formal cause that counts.[10]

Thank you again for so many fine, good books, which we (many of my friends and I) like too much to wish them invulnerable to attack—if, indeed, any book exists at which certain people cannot take pot shots. . . .[11]

É. GILSON

[1] The title of the first two editions was *De la connaissance de Dieu*, a brief work published at the request of Father Pierre Chaillet by Éditions du Témoignage chrétien (1945 and 1948). This short book, enlarged, had just been published by Aubier under another title, *Sur les chemins de Dieu*. It was Father General J. Janssens who invited me to attempt this task. The new edition bore no change in its basic purpose. It contained some amplifications, some new citations, and an afterword in which I warned the reader, with supporting explanations, that I disagreed with the broadsides launched at the preceding edition. *Sur les chemins de Dieu* would be reedited, throughout the sixties, and slightly abridged in the "Foi vivante" pocket series; then the unabridged edition was published in 1983 (Cerf, Traditions chrétiennes series). My Provincial, with whom I had shared this letter from Gilson, wrote to me on July 7: "I am overjoyed with Étienne Gilson's opinions."

[2] A.-D. Sertillanges, O.P. (1863–1948). See, for example, his *Les Sources de la croyance en Dieu* (1905), a monumental work which concludes with a paragraph entitled "L'inconnaissable divin"; he cites Saint Thomas, *De Veritate* 2, 1, ad 9: "The supreme knowledge we can attain in this life about God is to know that he is above everything we think about him." *Saint Thomas d'Aquin* (1910), vol. 1: 275–278. *Les Grandes Thèses de la philosophie thomiste* (1928). *Le Christianisme et les philosophies* (1932), vol. 1: 7. See also his commentary on the *Summa Theologiae* (ed. *Revue des jeunes*), "Dieu", vols. 2 and 3. Sertillanges refused to use the word "symbolism", tainted as it was at that time with subjectivism and "disguised agnosticism". He is cited several times in *Sur les chemins de Dieu*. Cf. É. Gilson, *Introduction à la philosophie chrétienne* (Vrin, 1960), 64.

In the conclusion of *Saint Thomas d'Aquin*, vol. 2, on the "future of Thomism", Sertillanges insisted that "thought is always a universal collaboration" and asked, "Does anyone think that he [Saint Thomas] would have rubbed shoulders with a Descartes, a Leibniz, a Spinoza, a Kant, or twenty others, without being affected by them in any way?" (pp. 330, 333). On May 10, 1910, he wrote to Father Laberthonnière: "My *Saint Thomas* has come out. . . . I have tried to make it a concourse for widely differing philosophies of education so that, going in one direction by means of works of this kind and coming from the other direction by means of works of the kind you publish, they might perhaps be able to arrive at a better understanding of one another" (in M.-T. Perrin, *Laberthonnière et ses amis* [Beauchesne, 1975], 213). In the *Annales* (December 1909): 255, *Testis* [= Blondel] had praised the Thomism of Sertillanges and Rousselot. Sertillanges and Gilson shared a mutual admiration for Bergson. Having published in 1941 a popular work, *Henri Bergson et le catholicisme*, which was considered too soft on Bergson, Sertillanges was to follow it with a corrective, *Lumière et périls du bergsonisme*, in the form of a letter "to our young philosophers" (Flammarion), in which one can read: "It is every bit as strategically necessary for our national Revolution (for us philosophers) to be guided by Saint Thomas as it was for the French Revolution to be led by its own "brilliant Commander-in-Chief" (pp. 24–26). Cf. L. 16, n. 4 (L. = letter; n. = note). Again in 1963, Gilson would consider Sertillanges the most authentic Thomist of the preceding generation (cf. Shook, *Gilson*, 366).

[3]This is the thesis that Gilson will constantly maintain, both as a historian and at the same time as a Thomistic philosopher and as a Christian. His letter expresses, doubtless intentionally, an agreement with the thought of *Surnaturel* (1946), as much as and even more than with *Sur les chemins de Dieu*. In *Le Philosophe et la théologie*, he likewise would write, referring to the criticisms formerly raised against Thomism by Péguy: "It is sad but true that the Thomism of his time lacked vigor, but it was not the

Thomism of Saint Thomas but rather the Thomism of the Thomists. . . . I don't know of a freer, tougher theology than that of Saint Thomas; neither do I know of any theology scoffers have more ruthlessly domesticated." On the root of the problem, he explains his views at length in his definitive work, *L'Être et l'Essence* (Vrin, 1948). In a note on pages 175–176, regarding the "influence of Wolff on modern scholasticism", he observes that "one can see it acting even upon the philosophical exegesis of Thomism itself. See, for example, R. Garrigou-Lagrange, *Dieu, son existence et sa nature. Solution thomiste des antinomies agnostiques*, 3rd ed. (Paris, Beauchesne, 1920), 170–179, in which the 'principle of the reason-for-being', according to which 'every being has a sufficient reason', finds itself tied in with the principle of identity by means of a reduction to the impossible and, in this sense, is turned into an analytical principle. Those who reason otherwise, he assures us (p. 175), separate themselves from 'traditional philosophy'. Yes, they do indeed separate themselves from what traditional philosophy has become since the time of Leibniz and Wolff, but what they are separated from is the exact opposite of the philosophy of Saint Thomas Aquinas." In spite of Garrigou-Lagrange's objection (in *Angelicum*, 1949: 321–322), the note was preserved in the second edition, revised and augmented, of 1962, p. 179.

In his numerous writings on the subject from 1907 to 1949, Garrigou-Lagrange leaned heavily on the *Précis de philosophie* by A. Penjon, who was himself a follower of the German A. Spir, whose *Pensée et Réalité* (Leipzig, 1873) Penjon had translated (Paris, 1896)—cf. Raymond Laverdière, *Le Principe de causalité, recherches thomistes récentes* (Vrin, 1969), 73–79; and the preface by P. M. D. Chenu, pp. 7–9: there occurred around 1900 "an infiltration of thought emanating from a different source of inspiration, into the very warp and woof of the School; namely, the introduction of

Wolff's philosophy. . . . The acceptance given to this peculiar aberration . . . has been surprising. . . ." Cf. L. 9, n. 8.

[4] The Franciscan Guillaume de la Mare, having written about 1278 a critique of Thomism entitled *Correctorium fratris Thomae*, brought on himself a rebuttal called *Correctorium corruptorii fratris Thomae*. Hence Gilson's snide application of this term to Cajetan's great commentary on the *Summa*, a commentary rather too generally held to be the norm of fidelity to Saint Thomas' thought. (Cajetanus = Thomas de Vio, O.P. [1469–1534], Master-General of the Order in 1508, Cardinal in 1517. His enormous commentary on the *Summa Theologiae*, completed in 1522, was later included, by order of Leo XIII, in the Pope's own monumental edition of the *Summa*, with the text of Cajetan's commentary printed in the form of a border around every page.) The author of *Correctorium corruptorii fratris Thomae* (about 1282), formerly considered to be Gilles de Rome, was actually an English Dominican "according to all appearances Richard Clapwell". Undoubtedly Richard Clapwell was inspired by Saint Thomas himself, for Saint Thomas used an analogous expression in referring to Averroës as a commentator on Aristotle, in his *De unitate intellectus*, chap. 4, ad finem: *"Non tam fuit Peripateticus, quam Peripateticae philosophiae depravator."* Cf. Mandonnet, O.P., *Siger de Brabant*, 2nd ed. (Louvain, 1911), 1:158; 2:xxviii.

Their appreciation of Cajetan's work is one of the central points on which Gilson and Maritain did not agree. Maritain, Prince Wladimir Ghika wrote in 1923, "recognized fidelity to the tradition of Saint Thomas and authentic kinship to the master's teaching only in such commentators as Bañez, Cajetan, John of Saint Thomas, the Schoolmen of Salamanca" ("Jacques Maritain", in *Documentation catholique* 2[1923]: col. 656). The three other "commentators" cited by Ghika themselves draw upon Cajetan. Maritain had indeed just written in 1921: "The School founded by Saint Thomas counted among its members some very famous names in the sixteenth and seventeenth centuries: Cajetan . . . , John of Saint Thomas, the Carmelite Fathers of Salamanca. . . . A living system of thought has never been known to stop growing. . . . Among the great Thomists, the master's thought, far from being engraved in stone, develops, becomes a living thing continually evolving and perfecting itself. Many intelligent people, victims of romantic scornfulness, never grasp this fact, really so easy to understand—with regard to the commentators", *Théonas ou Les Entretiens d'un sage et de deux philosophes sur diverses matières inégalement actuelles* (Nouvelle Librairie nationale), 174. (In answer to *Théonas*, Blondel published, in 1922, *Le Procès de l'intelligence*: cf. Blondel and Valensin, *Correspondance*, 3:91: letter of February 3, 1922. On the word "intelligence" in the *Revue universelle* of that time: the letter of June 15, 1920; ibid., 75. On the different meanings of the word "intellectualism" between 1900 and 1940: 2:18–22.) On the other hand, Maritain encountered Father Pedro Descoqs, S.J. (cf. L. 2, n. 2), in whose eyes Cajetan was worthy to pave the way for Suarez. Father Descoqs was to write in 1938, in *Le Mystère de notre élévation surnaturelle* (Beauchesne), 132: "Undoubtedly Cajetan is not infallible, either in matters of history, or of philosophy, or of theology. But when all is said and done, Cajetan is Cajetan, whatever one may think of some, or even many, of his theories; a metaphysician and a theologian of the first order, most certainly one of the greatest of the Thomistic School. . . . His exposition provides one of the simplest and most natural keys to interpreting Saint Thomas' thought. This thought, indeed, if it is confined to the several truly antinomic texts in which it is expressed, would appear to diverge into two irreducible trends. . . . On the contrary, in the way Cajetan understands it, it appears perfectly coherent and intelligible."

There is no doubt that the "commentator" assigned another orientation to his master's work. Cf. H. de Lubac, *Augustinisme et théologie moderne* (Aubier, 1965). See below, L. 6.

[5] Like Sertillanges, Gilson was amply cited in *Sur les chemins de Dieu*. Perhaps he may not have noticed the attempt to establish more firmly, in chapters 2 and 5 ("De l'affirmation de Dieu" and "De l'ineffabilité de Dieu"), the radical affirmation which continually motivates and directs every aspect of "apophatic theology" (*Deus semper major*) and which prevents it from ever turning into denial. It is perhaps an analogous approach that Gilson himself was to suggest when he wrote in October 1970, in the third draft of his short work, *L'Athéisme difficile*: "The affirmation of God is not necessarily tied in with innatism . . . , but it seems impossible to avoid the modicum of innatism required by the nature of first principles and that in any case holds the relationship between the notions of God and being to be mystery" (posthumous edition by H. Gouhier [Vrin, 1974], 62). On the "Negative Way" of the Pseudo-Dionysius, Father Michel Corbin has recently reopened the subject, vindicating the fully Christian character of Dionysius' thought by means of a very tightly constructed dialectic (*Revue des sciences philosophiques et théologiques*, 1985).

In his *Sermon sur la mort* (at the Louvre, March 22, 1622), Bossuet expressed himself in nearly the same way: ". . . Don't you feel that there comes from the depths of our souls a celestial light which drives away all those shades, so delicate and ephemeral that we might have imagined them? And if . . . you were to ask what that light is, a voice would rise from the center of the soul saying: I do not know what it is, but notwithstanding, it isn't *that*. What strength, what energy, what hidden power does this soul feel within itself, correcting it, contradicting it, and even daring to reject everything the soul thinks? . . ." (see the whole passage, cited by Blondel, "XV<sup>e</sup> centenaire de la mort de saint Augustin", *Revue de métaphysique et de morale*, 1930: 438–439, note).

At the end of the second edition of *L'Être et l'Essence*, 365–378, Gilson observes that "no one has spoken more eloquently than Heidegger about the anguish of thought face-to-face with pure being. Saint Thomas, less of a romantic but speaking in the same sense, said of intellect forcing itself to go beyond the plane of being and essence, that intellect 'then finds itself in a sort of confusion'. Intellect is not happy in this confused state; it suffers. This anguish, which brings on mental giddiness, so takes hold of a man that he, the only one of all creatures capable of doing so, posits this marvel of marvels: 'that being, *is*'. But that's nothing new. . . . Not without reason did Saint Thomas place apophatic theology, in its highest form, at the pinnacle of meditation on God and being. Anguish in the face of pure being is perhaps nothing more than another name for the fear of God. . . ." Then, recalling the major texts of Saint Thomas on the question (*De ente et essentia, In Boethium de Trinitate*), Gilson applies to Heidegger what Saint Thomas said about the classical philosophers: "*In quo satis apparet quantam angustiam patiebantur hinc inde eorum praeclara ingenia*" (*Contra Gentiles* III, 49). "For there are good reasons why reason shrinks from this point of direct contact with the solidity of being. Likewise God, whose name this solidity of being bears, is one we can apprehend only as unknown, '*quod quidem contingit dum de eo quid non sit cognoscimus, quid vero sit penitus manet ignotum*'. Let Martin Heidegger be assured that even among the most fervent Thomists, he will find very few who take this expression *penitus ignotum* literally. Moses was the only one of his people who entered into the midst of the cloud: '*Unde et ad hujus sublimissimae cognitionis ignorantiam demonstrandam, de Moyse dicitur*, Ex. 20, 21, *quod accessit ad caliginem in qua est Deus*' (pp. 375–377)."

What Gilson endeavored to define as a philosopher, Claudel expressed as a poet. A joyous echo of the above biblical allusion, Claudel's "*oui*" is addressed to the inexhaustible Being, and so that the echo can continue to resound, the poet enters upon the Negative Way (a Way which is not one of denial, but, as Maurice Blondel said, one of "elimination"): "Don't we have a right *not* to see God? By all those ways in which I do not know him, I can recognize him!" And in yet another form: "Thou hast given us night after day, and hard truth in the dark night sky." Cf. H. de Lubac, "Claudel théologien" in *Théologies d'occasion* (Paris: DDB, 1984), 466.

[6] Already Hervé Nedellec, O.P. (Herveus Natalis), who was Master-General of the Order in 1318, and through whose influence every Dominican was to become a Thomist, who had even written a *Correctorium fratris Jacobi Metenis* (Jacques de Metz) against his fellow-Dominican for not having been faithful enough to Saint Thomas, had himself drawn away from the master "on three principal points", by rejecting the "structure of being and essence within finite being" (É. Gilson, *Les tribulations de Sophie* [Vrin, 1967], 21-22; *La Philosophie au Moyen Age*, 2nd ed. [1952], 543–544 and 621–622). As a consequence quite a few more doctrinal adulterations were to emerge. No one knew better than Gilson "how to be on guard against the hybrid character of certain presentations of Thomism that were current at the beginning of the twentieth century, a time when heavy doses of Suarezianism and Bañezianism (not to mention Wolff and Descartes . . .) and Scotism besides, to be precise, were being introduced": Fernand Guimet, "Actualité de Duns Scot", in *Recherches de philosophie*, no. 2 (DDB, 1956), 320. In *Philosophe et théologie*, 67–68, Gilson gives another example of this kind of Thomists, as vapid as they were stubborn: Father Pègues held that the political doctrine of Maurras was the same as Saint Thomas'; but "one has only to open the *Summa*

33

*Theologiae* at the right place to know that this is not true";
however, "this theologian [Pègues] was not the only one
who made this mistake. . . . How on earth, by what esoteric
lines of reasoning could Thomistic philosophy seem to them
to provide a theological justification for the political doctrine
of Maurras? It certainly is evident that these individuals had
a vested interest in their claim. It would be nice to know
exactly what truth of 'Thomism' in particular it must have
been that could be interpreted to admit of such selective
affinities with a positivism which, like that of Comte, took
a lively interest in Rome but cared nothing for Jerusalem".
(In 1927, the Rev. Victor Bouillon dedicated a book on "The
Political Thought of Saint Thomas" to Charles Maurras.)

For his part, on February 13, 1922, Blondel had written
from Aix to his friend Wehrlé: "Father Pègues gave an incredible lecture Thursday entitled 'Politique d'abord' [Politics
first], glorifying absolutism, the Inquisition and Maurras"
(Blondel and Wehrlé, *Correspondance* [Aubier, 1969], 2:560).
Besides his huge *Commentaire littéral de la Somme théologique*
(from 1907 to 1928), Father Pègues published *La Somme
théologique en forme de catéchisme pour tous les fidèles* [The *Summa
Theologiae* in the form of a catechism for all the faithful], a
*Catéchisme extrait de Saint Thomas pour les écoles* [A catechism
drawn from Saint Thomas for grammar schools], and an
*Extrait du catéchisme de saint Thomas pour les tout-petits* [A little
catechism from Saint Thomas for small children] (1921). The
first part of his *Initiation thomiste* was devoted to "who taught
Saint Thomas", that is to say, the philosophers, the writers
of Holy Scripture, the Church Fathers, the Doctors of the
Church, and the Church herself. In the course of the winter
of 1922–1923, I was writing from Aix to Father Fessard: "Do
you know, the cultural level at Aix has hit rock bottom! M.
Blondel is silent. But the worst misfortune is not that he was
replaced in the department [of Philosophy] by Goblot. The
worst thing is that all the Catholics in town have been going,

for two weeks now, to the Salle du Cercle Saint-Mitre, to hear . . . Father Pègues. . . . I want to go listen to him at least once, next Thursday. As for Blondel, to think that only last winter he was giving his public lecture series on 'Saint Augustine and Today's Problems in Philosophy'! Everywhere I go I see the posters announcing those lectures still hanging up, as if to scoff at me."

[7] "Returning to the real Saint Thomas": this was also, as Gilson accurately perceived, my clearly expressed (and I believe always well-founded) intention, whether in *Sur les chemins de Dieu* or in *Surnaturel*. I wrote, in 1957, to a Thomist theologian whose good will was beyond question: "I am rather astonished that you would make me appear opposed to Saint Thomas from one end to the other, since, at least in most instances and on all basic points, my analyses hardly do more than put Saint Thomas into French." Two rudimentary remarks Gilson made which date from the fifties were, at that time, particularly germane: "The fact that an author professes to be a follower of Saint Thomas creates a presumption in favor of his Thomism, but it does not constitute proof of it, especially if he is a member of the Dominican Order, in which fidelity to Saint Thomas early became the official party line" (*La Philosophie du Moyen Age*, 545); and "The method which consists in deducing what theologians of yesteryear must have said in order to have spoken the truth sometimes makes it as difficult to interpret Saint Thomas as it is to interpret Saint Augustine" ("Église et Cité de Dieu chez saint Augustin", in *Archives d'histoire doctrinale et littéraire du Moyen Age*, 20, année 1953 [Vrin, 1954]: 17, note).

[8] This allusion to the imperfection of the "language", it will be noted, is repeated at the end of the letter. Later, Gilson will express himself otherwise. Cf. Letters 5, 6, 7, 8.

[9] This was the essential thesis of *Surnaturel*, in contrast to the previously mentioned theories of "pure nature", systematized in the sixteenth and seventeenth centuries and

adopted from then on by the majority of Catholic schools of theology, even those most opposed to one another. Cajetan can be identified as their principal initiator in his *Commentary on the Summa Theologica of St. Thomas.* For my own interpretations, before the agreement manifested by Gilson in these letters, I had obtained, among others, the concurrence of Dom Cappuyns, a Benedictine of Mont César (Louvain) who, in a long survey in the *Bulletin de théologie ancienne et médiévale*, catalogued most masterfully all the publications over the past twenty-five years on the history of the theology of the supernatural: "The exegesis . . . of the texts of Saint Thomas is as enlightening as it is conclusive. It is the interpretation held today rather generally among historians of Thomistic thought. . . ." None of the numerous theologians who attacked my work seemed to have known about Dom Cappuyns' opinion. Cf. L. 8, n. 1.

[10]In a discourse on "Thomism and Its Present Situation" (Italy, April 1965), Gilson was to repeat the two major examples cited in this letter, of the infidelity of modern Thomists to their master: "Allow me to put to you two propositions of Saint Thomas Aquinas that are difficult to bring up without provoking protests on the part of certain souls who are priggish about their orthodoxy. The first, on which there have been endless controversies, is that 'every intellect naturally desires to behold the divine Essence'. Just mention this proposition in good theological circles, and you'll see what will happen to you. I am not saying: propose this proposition as true, but simply as expressing the authentic thought of Saint Thomas. Nevertheless, it really is he who said: '*Omnis intellectus naturaliter desiderat divinae substantiae visionem . . .*'" (*Contra Gentiles* I, 3, 57, 4).

"Here's a second example of an experiment which is bound to succeed. At any meeting of Catholic philosophers and theologians, even Thomists, just try saying that what God is remains completely unknown to us: you may be assured of immediately hearing yourself accused of agnosticism. Things won't go any better for you if you say: I know that we know God exists; I'm saying only that what God is, is unknown to us, even completely unknown. They will repeat that you are an agnostic and you will never be able to clear yourself of the accusation. So be it, but what it is impossible for me to deny is that this is indeed the teaching of Saint Thomas Aquinas . . .: '*quid vero sit (Deus),* penitus *manet incognitum* . . .' (*Contra Gentiles* I, 3, 49, 7)." (*Les tribulations de Sophie,* 22–24.) Cf. Henry Bars, *Maritain et son temps* (Grasset, 1959), 325: "Saint Thomas explicitly refuses us the knowledge of the divine Essence in this life '*secundum quod in se est*': from this formula and from others like it, Father Sertillanges developed an exegesis which Gilson termed 'provocative' and Maritain judged 'completely equivocal' (*Degrés du savoir* [1932], 841). Maritain, for his part, seemed to Gilson perhaps a bit too 'careful to keep from us any knowledge of the divine Essence'" (*Le Thomisme,* 200, n. 2). They could have come nearer agreement, it seems to me, if both of them had had recourse to the language of Saint Augustine. Cf. the *Confessions* 1, I, 4, 4, etc.

[11] On July 18, I wrote to Father Fontoynont: "This book, *Sur les chemins de Dieu,* earned me an astonishing letter from Étienne Gilson. . . . Into the bargain, he agrees with the thought of *Surnaturel,* which he would like to see done all over again in the same way. But above all, this letter is a violent blast at the official theologians. . . . He doesn't do things by halves! Of course, he's a layman; he's old, worn out, deprived of titles he truly deserves. I had a certain pleasure in reading that letter; but what a stir it would create if I were to give that letter too much publicity!"

9, rue Saint-Romain, Paris VI<sup>e</sup>

May 21, 1960

Reverend and dear Father,

Thank you very much for your splendid letter.[1]
I don't often get letters like that! I'm going to
reread it and meditate on it to my heart's content.
Meanwhile, let me assure you, it has never entered
my mind to fret about being a Thomist *secundum
voluntatem Petri*, as Father Descoqs[2] was so keen
on doing. On that subject I have some rather
specific texts which I decided not to put forward
because I don't think he would have wanted it.
His official position, the stand he has taken publicly, is the same one he's always defended (sometimes ranting and raving, against Maritain),[3] in
the *Archives de philosophie*: namely, that the papacy
has never, in any way, shape, or form, required
acceptance of any interpretation of Thomism that
would contradict or preclude the Suarezian view.[4]
His published opinions on this matter are so
mulish that I haven't even bothered to quote them.

You know, when you *say* something, it means one thing; but when you publish it, it can acquire another meaning altogether. Father Laberthonnière wrote that Saint Thomas did the Church more harm than Luther did; he *said* that, but we can hold him responsible for it because he published it.[5] He once said to me, speaking of Saint Thomas: "I hate him; he's a troublemaker." But he didn't print this remark, so I can't allow myself to discuss it in the public press. Father Teilhard de Chardin asked me, when we were attending the hundredth anniversary of Columbia University at Arden House, near New York City: "Tell me, who's going to expound to us this 'religionless Christianity' we've all been waiting to hear about?" I was dumbfounded, the more so because that very afternoon I had observed him, completely absorbed in the reading of his Office. People are complex. But, after all, if he doesn't publish that remark himself, I have no business publishing it. In any case where a comment might do damage, I believe this is the proper code of conduct to follow.[6]

On the root of the problem, I'll try to explain myself shortly. I think you can be a Scotist, a Suarezian,[7] even a follower of Cajetan without contravening pontifical directives,[8] because all other theologies are capable of at least tacitly embodying the Thomism of Saint Thomas. Saint Thomas himself adhered to many other theologians' teachings. What I spend so much time explaining to my friends who claim to draw their inspiration from other theologies, is that it's perfectly all right to cling to another system as long as you don't use your pet theology to oppose Saint Thomas'. They all do it. And they themselves, no less than certain people who call themselves Thomists, are fanatics too.[9] They are trying to prove, not just that Duns Scotus was right, but that Saint Thomas was wrong, as if the one were a logical consequence of the other. Who among us would want to turn his back on Saint Augustine's heritage to go along with Saint Thomas? Saint Thomas himself stoutly refused to do such a thing.[10] It is intrinsically simple—so very simple that it is almost impossible to explain it to anyone.

Don't worry. We need you, and please be sure of my warmest good wishes and deep respect.

É. GILSON

---

[1] What was this letter all about? For the life of me, I can't remember. Perhaps it was a note of thanks, adding some reflections, for his *Introduction à la philosophie chrétienne* (1960), or rather, maybe, for *Le Philosophe et la théologie*. This latter work, written in a slightly paradoxical style, was something in the line of an intellectual autobiography, and according to Shook, *Gilson*, 347, not very well received by a certain

number of influential theologians. Its title seemed to suggest that philosophy ought to lead to faith and theology, whereas Gilson's thought was somewhat the reverse. The title had been chosen by Daniel-Rops, who had engaged Gilson to write the book for Fayard to publish in their "Le Signe" series. Gilson would have preferred the title, "Le théologien et la philosophie", which would have avoided misunderstandings. "Not a lucky book", I think I said to Shook in 1974. In any case, it is a very alert and stimulating volume whose last three chapters explain "Christian philosophy" in about the same way as Leo XIII understood it in the encyclical *Aeterni patris* in 1879, as "the development of progress from a truth which in itself is not susceptible of progress".

[2]Pedro Descoqs, 1877–1946; philosophy professor in the Jesuit Scholasticate on the island of Jersey; co-founder in 1922 of the *Archives de philosophie*, whose first secretary was Father J. Souilhé, philosophy professor in the Jesuit Scholasticate of Vals près Le Puy (a Plato specialist); the *Archives de philosophie* published, among other writings of Descoqs: *Thomisme et scolastique, à propos de M. Rougier* (1927; 2nd ed., 1935). In his youth, as an active sympathizer with Action française, he wrote (Études, September 5, 1909): "Can't the results themselves be used as a basis for dialogue? . . . There is a 'social dynamic' on which an atheist and a believer can be in perfect agreement. [. . . The Catholic atheist] holds nothing dearer than to cause the Church to triumph, if not among souls, at least in society. And however little that may seem, isn't half a loaf better than no bread at all?" In 1910, in *La Semaine sociale de Bordeaux et le monophorisme* (articles from the *Annales de philosophie chrétienne*, collected and published as a booklet), *Testis* reacted violently to these opinions. Descoqs then stubbornly averred that Blondel was collaborating with atheists since the rector of his university (Aix), M. Payot, was one (cf. René Virgoulay, *Blondel et le modernisme* [Cerf, 1980], 445-473). In 1911, Descoqs reprinted his

41

articles from *Études* in one volume: *À travers l'oeuvre de Charles Maurras*, plus *Monophorisme et Action française*, which is a reply to *Testis*. The major portion of the work is a critique of Maurras' system, whose "insufficiency" and "gaps" Descoqs deplored; however, he considered its "political conclusions" to be "correct", even though he felt they lacked "the necessary finishing touches": "the natural order as viewed by Maurras, far from being opposed to the supernatural order, is in perfect accord with it"; thus, there is no danger in Maurras for "the healthy mind". The author ends by mentioning his admiration for *L'Avenir de l'intelligence*, which had been recently published; if he regrets that "its inspiration is still so limited", he recognizes its merit "with interest".

In that same year, 1911, Father Laberthonnière, who had already criticized Descoqs' articles in 1910 in the *Annales de philosophie chrétienne*, published an aggressive pamphlet: *Autour de l'*'*Action française*', soon to be followed by a thicker volume: *Positivisme et catholicisme, à propos de l'*'*Action française*'. In 1913, Descoqs' work came out in its third edition. Laberthonnière, who had by then been forbidden to teach or to publish, reacted in a letter of August 28 to Édouard Le Roy: "Father Descoqs, flaunting his title 'professor in the Jesuit Scholasticate', is putting out in two volumes a new edition of his book on Maurras, treating me I'll leave you to guess how, and being more of a cynical casuist than all the Escobars of the past lumped together . . ." (Perrin, *Laberthonnière*, 280-281). But a friend who read the book was able to pick out "an almost prophetic page where his humility triumphs over his admiration. Noting the absolute hold a master has over the disciples in his school, Father Descoqs asks himself what would happen if, some day, the Church were to disapprove of this movement. With an orthodoxy somewhat less easily offended than other people's, he then showed himself to be a most devoted and obedient son of the Catholic Church" (G. Picard, "In memoriam,

le Père Pedro Descoqs", *Archives de philosophie* 18, 1 [1949]:
129–135).

"All his life, he scrapped with the 'so-called Thomistic
School'. As a true Norman, he was a litigious squabbler, he
was always planning something against somebody or other
. . ., he was incessantly finding some petty Thomist to put
in his place"; his attacks were aimed at two forms of neo-
Thomism: the first, one which according to him "interpreted
the master's thought unsubtly and attempted to use it as an
impenetrable barrier against all manner of philosophical progress"; the second, one which he accused of "treason" to Saint
Thomas "because it transposed his formulae into idealism":
these were Rousselot, J. Maréchal, Guy de Broglie, whose
"pretense of rationalism and naturalism was not only dam-
nable but condemned already"; everywhere he hounded the
"presumptuous rationalist theologies" and the "systematic
mind"; however, Father Picard adds, he maintained "a frank
and cordial rapport with the very ones whose ideas he fought"
(Ibid.).

Works of Father Descoqs: *Essai sur l'hylémorphisme* )1924);
*Institutiones metaphysicae generalis*, vol. 1 (1925); *Praelectiones
theologiae naturalis*, I (1932); II (1935); *Le Mystère de notre élévation surnaturelle* (1938); *Schema theodiceae* (1941); *Autour de
la crise du transformisme* (1944). I was Father Descoqs' student
on Jersey in 1922 and 1923.

[3] This quarrel about obedience had been going on for centuries. It had broken out again after the encyclical *Aeterni
patris* of Leo XIII (1879). In a popular work, *Le Docteur
angélique* (Paris: DDB, 1930), chapter 4, "Le Docteur commun", Maritain had rehashed the numerous documents of
the Roman magisterium exalting Saint Thomas' doctrine,
from John XXII (bull of canonization, 1323) to Pius IX and
Leo XIII; then, having stressed the statements of the three
latest Popes, Pius X, Benedict XV, and Pius XI, he concluded: "Does the Church impose upon the faithful any

43

'ideological conformity' as far as philosophy is concerned? No." Except this No was accompanied by a "but . . .". About 1914, the argument simultaneously heated up and narrowed its focus. On June 29, a *motu proprio* of Pius X ordered all centers of theological studies to incorporate into their curricula the *principia et pronunciata majora* of Saint Thomas. An influential group of Thomists who had boiled the saint's teachings down to twenty-four theses hastened to have their feat accepted and published by the Congregation of Studies on July 27 (*Acta Apostolicae Sedis* 6 [1914]: 383–386; their approval declared the twenty-four theses to be in conformity with Saint Thomas' principles but said nothing about making them a matter of obedience). On March 7, 1916, Father Matiussi, S.J., published a commentary on the twenty-four theses, first in the *Civiltà cattolica*, and then as a book (Turin; French translation in 1926; *Les Points fondamentaux de la philosophie thomiste*); followed by Father Pègues, O.P., in 1918: *Autour de saint Thomas, une controverse récente*. Cf. Édouard Hugon, O.P., *Les Vingt-Quatre Thèses thomistes* (1922). See also Paul Geny, "Saint Thomas, le maître par excellence", *Études*, January 1915; and, for Germany, Karl H. Neufeld, "Geschichte und Mensch, A. Delps", *Analecta Gregoriana* (Rome, 1983): 44–52. In 1943, J. Jugnet, in an appendix to *Pour connaître la pensée de saint Thomas* (published by Bordas), on "L'Église et le thomisme", made reference to Maritain (and to Garrigou-Lagrange).

[4] As far as that went, Father Descoqs was probably more correct than Gilson seems to think here. The militant "Thomists", who were not above putting pressure on the Holy See, were attaching excessive significance to the pontifical texts while systematically ignoring certain compensating texts. Others, such as Cardinal Mercier and Father Sertillanges, disapproved of this overkill. On March 19, 1917, the Father-General of the Jesuits, Vladimir Ledochowski, had addressed to the members of the Society a long letter *De*

*doctrina S. Thomae magis magisque in societate fovenda*, prefaced by a letter of approval from Benedict XV. "*Recte nos sensisse arbitramur*", the Pope wrote, "*cum eos putasti Angelico Doctore satis adhaerere, qui universas de Thomae doctrina theses perinde proponendas censeant, ac tutas ad dirigendum normas, nullo scilicet omnium amplectendarum thesium imposito officio.*" After several broad historical sketches on the relationships between Christian faith and philosophy since the time of the Fathers of the Church, the Father-General enumerated the innovative characteristics of Saint Thomas' work, whose example showed how "*in tractandis Ecclesiae Doctorum effatis magna reverentia cum modesta libertate ad progressum scientiae necessarie conjungenda sunt*"; he mentioned various famous Thomists: Herveus Natalis, Cajetan, Soto, the Schoolmen of Salamanca, all of whom had considered the act of approving all his theses without weighing them carefully to be contrary to the very spirit of their master; Father Ledochowski criticized the over-protective texts of Leo XIII and reclaimed for all a "healthy freedom". He cited the eulogy for Suarez by Cardinal Zéphirin Zigliara, O.P., calling Suarez "perhaps the most eminent embodiment of Scholastic philosophy since Saint Thomas' time", etc. He ended by saying that an absolute unity of thought is neither necessary nor useful, that the Church has never required it; that, besides, it could never be attained, because the "*captatio*" of this unhelpful and fallacious concept exposes charity, knowledge, and even the Faith to the gravest dangers (*Acts romana S.J.*, 2:318–352). On June 29, 1923, in his encyclical *Studiorum ducem*, Pius XI reacted as Benedict XV had done, with his customary energy: "*At ne quid eo amplius alii ab aliis exigant, quam quod ab omnibus exigit omnium magistra et mater Ecclesia*" (*Acta Apostolicae Sedis* 15, n. 7, 5.7 [1923]: 324).

In his *Institutiones Metaphysicae* (1925), 80–94, Father Descoqs considers the matter "*de speciali auctoritate S. Thomae*".

On the business of the "twenty-four theses", Benedict XV's

conciliatory statement, its official incorporation into the *Epitome Instituti Societatis Jesu*, Father Guido Matiussi's activism to the contrary, together with the 1926 French translation of his work by Father Jean Levillain, who in turn found support in the opinions of Father Le Rohellec, C.S.Sp., Father Boyer, S.J., and J. Maritain, etc.—see Blondel and Valensin, *Correspondance*, text annotated by H. de Lubac (Aubier, 1965), 3:101–104. On July 27, 1923, Blondel had written to Valensin: "The Society of Jesus, too often straying from the path of authentic doctrine and bowing beneath the widening yoke of a neo-Thomism (as different, besides, from Saint Thomas' theology as Jansen's is from Saint Augustine's), is turning itself over, bound hand and foot, to a dictatorship which will tend to become ever more oppressive. . . ." In these prophetic terms, for which the frankness of a personal letter is explanation enough, Blondel was being critical of an abuse that was really, in spite of Pius XI's renewed intervention, going to become even worse. See also his long letter to X, dated June 20, 1928, with a copy to his friend the Rev. Wehrlé: "I have often noticed that those who presume to impose their own definition of Thomism upon others are the very people who least understand Saint Thomas' thought, and who are at the same time most deficient in philosophical and Christian sensitivity. . . . I consider myself more of a Thomist than a lot of strict neo-Scholastics (etc.). . . . I would never get done, if I tried to list all the clashes that make the idea of an orthodox Thomism so hard to pin down, even though it has been defined by Councils and Popes as the only true and correct Catholic teaching" (Blondel and Wehrlé, *Correspondance* 2:646–649). These reflections seem to me to accord well with perceptions Gilson will articulate more than once.

Again in 1946, at the end of a long string of accusations, Father Garrigou-Lagrange was to blame the errors he thought he had uncovered in the works of several Jesuit writers, on the (supposed) fact that they did not adhere to the "twenty-four theses" (*Angelicum* 23:142, n. 9). According to Giuseppe Alberigo, one of the statements that Father Chenu, O.P., was asked to sign in Rome in 1938 "implies that he was accused of non-observance of the twenty-four theses" (M. D. Chenu, *Une école de théologie, le Saulchoir* [Cerf; repr. 1985], 18). Cf. L. 6, n. 10.

[5]Two observations are essential for understanding what Gilson is saying here: (1) the "Thomism" that Laberthonnière had absorbed at seminary was far from being the real thing, and indeed was of the same kind he was later to oppose so bitterly, without ever having had the time or, certainly, the inclination to make a thorough reexamination of Thomism for himself (further, he was more of a moral philosopher than a metaphysician). Cf. the testimony Gilson offers, speaking from experience, in *Philosophe et théologie*, 49–64; (2) in the first third of the twentieth century, this "Thomism" seemed to be closely allied with the Action française movement, which included both Thomists who considered themselves to be "of the strict obedience" and Suarezian Thomists, who had cemented themselves into a powerful "Scholastic" bloc, despite recurrent infighting. Again, this is what Gilson notes, pp. 66–69: ". . . When Father Laberthonnière took Father Pedro Descoqs to task about his chapter on Action française, I didn't doubt for an instant that his fate was sealed. . . . I remember that I was not alone in predicting this. Father Laberthonnière published, in 1911, a slim pamphlet of forty-two pages: *Autour de l' 'Action française'*; his friends always believed that his enemies never forgave him for it." Cf. Virgoulay, *Blondel et modernisme*, 252–254. The exceptionally harsh punishment of being forbidden to teach or to publish could only have exacerbated any bias in his attitude or touchiness in his temperament. But he was in no way a "modernist" and his obedience was heroic. "For my part", Gilson concludes after calling to mind what was to him the "conflict between Greek rationalism and Christian faith", "I saw above

47

all a priest who had had his soul torn to pieces by the very Church that his zeal for the Church had forced him to oppose, a priest who was suffering. . . . It was not surprising that the placing of some of his writings on the Index, later followed by the cruel prohibition from teaching and publishing, had driven his friends wild. . . . Even in this isolation, I never heard him utter a single rebellious word, nor the least complaint. His submission to the Church was exemplary . . ., he never ceased to urge his friends to have patience and to bow respectfully to discipline" (ibid., 64). On Saint Thomas, he stood firm: "I say again to anyone who is willing to listen", he wrote to Blondel in 1922, "that the few citations I made from Saint Thomas to support my own conclusions were incorrect and I did wrong to quote them" (Bellevert, *Colloque*, 137; in the precise case to which he was referring, he had been absolutely right besides).

Gilson, as a young preparatory-school teacher, had met Father Laberthonnière fairly early on. He liked him. According to a letter to his mother, dated July 1908, he was then writing an aricle (that never saw print) for the *Annales de philosophie chrétienne*. What was this article, and why didn't it get published? Could its author have had a prudent second thought at the last minute, or rather, could his conscience have been beset by a deeper feeling of disillusionment with the magazine's leanings? What seems certain is that he did not care for the servile self-consciousness, to his mind quite out of proportion, manifested by the *Annales* in its approach to philosophy. Moreover, he thought it clumsy of Laberthonnière to have injected his dislike of Saint Thomas into the debate about Action française. Even then, too, Blondel had been making similar objections to his friend, gently but "speaking frankly". But Gilson was still less favorably disposed toward Blondel's frame of mind. He was not a proponent of what seemed to him a muddling of the subject-matter: history, philosophy, politics, religion. . . . And his own sympathies

lay more in the direction of the parliamentary socialism of
men like the Rev. Lemire, indeed the exegetical experimen-
talism of one like Loisy. At the death of Pius X, he breathed
a sigh of relief. "I hope", he wrote to his mother, "to feel
more at ease with his successor" (Shook, *Gilson*, 67), but
even that would not have been enough to reconcile him with
positions from which, on the contrary, he was drawing
further and further away.

On April 29, 1931, Monsignor Daniel Pézeril, then aged
nineteen, had a conversation with Father Laberthonnière. He
relates that Father Laberthonnière told him, about Gilson: "I
had showed him around the offices of the *Annales de
philosophie chrétienne*, when he was a young student; I used
to keep track of his progress with interest. After the war, he
came back from prison camp and invited me to attend a
lecture he was giving to a select group. I gladly accepted. In
fact, the whole thing was directed against me. . . ." "It is
clear", Monsignor Pézeril continues, "that for many reasons
there could hardly be any mutual understanding between the
argumentative Gilson and the intuitive Laberthonnière. This
is why I was touched that the professor in the Collège de
France, telling his own story of the incident and once again
rejecting Laberthonnière's opinions out of hand, nevertheless
pays him homage as a 'priest whose purity of life and whose
piety are examples to us all, a priest fighting for religion in
peril. . . .'" (Bellevert, *Colloque*, 240–241).
See "Colloque Laberthonnière, December 16–17, 1982",
in *Revue de l'Institut catholique de Paris*, Oct.–Dec. 1983.

[6] A wise rule. But in the case of Father Teilhard, Gilson
himself came to realize a little later that his remark was not
as "damaging" as he had first thought. Cf. L. 5 and 10.

[7] On Suarez: R. de Scoraille, S.J., *François Suarez*, 2 vol.
(1911); L. Mahieu, *Fr. Suarez, sa philosophie et les rapports
qu'elle a avec sa théologie* (1921); very critical. P. Descoqs,
*Institutiones metaphysicae* (1925), passim; R. Brouillard,

49

article "Suarez", *Dictionnaire de théologie catholique* 14.2 (1941); G. Picard, "Le thomisme de Suarez", *Archives de philosophie* 18.1 (1949): 108–128. For Father Picard, Suarez "belongs to the Thomistic School"; he presents therein a "particular nuance"; if Thomism were a cathedral, some people have said that Suarez could salvage all the separate stones, but that the cathedral would no longer be standing: "there is a kernel of truth in this criticism", because Suarez is "eclectic" and "is headed toward nominalism"; the Suarezian metaphysic is a "critical and analytical Thomism". Gilson roundly declares: "It is the antithesis of Thomism": his metaphysical thought "has being, as an abstraction derived from existence, for its object. . . . The Suarezians are wary of this *esse*, which they find difficult to define accurately. It is as essences, and only as essences, that created beings can become subjects of scientific study as we understand it. . . . What a strange science: the study of created things such that they *would be* even if they *did not exist!*" But at the same time, he observes that "the mistake made by many of their Thomist opponents is that of accepting the Suarezian notion of metaphysical knowledge and then immediately wanting to reject the Suarezian notion of being. If one admits, with Suarez, that essence is being itself, how can one combine it with whatever it is that creates being? That would be making essence into what it already is" (*Introduction à la philosophie chrétienne*, 94–95, 191).

A number of Thomists are also Suarezians (and there have been Suarezians since before the time of Suarez), by virtue of their idea of the double finality of the rational creature, an idea which is crystallized in the notion of a "state of pure nature". This is what Gilson also observes (cf. following letters). Thus Father Descoqs, *Monophorisme et Action française* (Beauchesne, 1913), 20–21: "The historic order in which we live includes our call to the beatific vision. . . . But does it follow that in the study of historical nature there is no reason to be concerned with the state of pure nature? . . . Does it follow that with Cajetan and Suarez no longing for the super-natural is admissible in natural nature . . . , or that, with other Doctors, there is recognized in natural nature only an ineffectual desire, a conditional will, a vague impulse . . . ?" Blaise Romeyer ("La théorie suarézienne d'un état de nature pure", *Archives de philosophie* 18.1 [1949]: 37–63) does his best to show that this theory does not represent a "laicization of the soul" but instead a "real progress of the faculty of reason", and that Blondel, by no means rejecting this theory, distinctly tries hard to bring to completion the philosophical efforts "of Suarez and many other Catholic thinkers".

[8] The solution does not always look that simple to us, when it is a question of systems made up of theses that are contradictory—except when speaking of basic understanding within one and the same faith. But Gilson seems to us to judge rightly when he refuses, under the pretext of being a Thomist, to "desert his Augustinian heritage". On that point we were always in complete unanimity. See below, Appendix II.

[9] Examples abound, in every sense. When, concerning an article on Aristotle and modern criticism (*Revue universelle*, November 1, 1921), Father Descoqs accused the author of "denying at the same time both the evidence and authentic Thomism" (*Institutiones metaphysicae*, 33), he gave in, as he did all too often, to the demon of contentiousness, as when he went after Blondel about Action française, for broaching "a subject which was beyond his competence"; or another time when he submitted to Father Laberthonnière that his criticism "showed such ignorance . . . that it would really be difficult to pay it any attention"—adding gratuitously, alluding to works recently placed on the Index: "He ought not to leave himself open to being reminded of such painful memories, which, moreover, we [Father Descoqs] would tactfully refrain from bringing up" (*Monophorisme et Action française* [1964], vi, viii). But he can hardly be blamed for having picked up on the following unfortunate choice of

words in regard to the Church and Saint Thomas' philosophy (1921): "God, in his noblest works, proceeds by privilege and . . . by special cases. Since he sent his Son into the world only once . . . , should it be so startling that he gave his Church only one Doctor par excellence in philosophical and theological wisdom?"

Between Gilson and Descoqs, the weapon of choice was the barb rather than the bomb. "We must confess", said Descoqs, "that we did not fully understand how the distinguished professor from the Sorbonne succeeded in . . ." (*Institutiones metaphysicae*, 539, n. 1). As for Gilson, he did not until somewhat later indulge in the malicious fun of dissecting, coolly and in measured phrases, Descoqs' strategy in the endless ecclesiastical debate on Thomism: ". . . He was a Suarezian. On the other hand, being a Jesuit, he was faithfully submissive to the directives of the Holy See. That made him a Thomist. But even this did not put him between a rock and a hard place. Not being able to make Suarez into a Thomist, he did what was needful to make Saint Thomas a Suarezian. To his last breath, this intelligent man, so fully informed on all manner of philosophies, this dialectician with a mind like a tightly-wound steel spring, stiffly upheld this monstrous conviction, not that the combination of essence and existence is an error, which would be merely a philosophical opinion, but in fact that *Saint Thomas himself never taught it*. He even had an unassailable syllogism behind this assertion: the Universal Doctor of the Church can never have taught anything absurd; but the combination of essence and existence is both contradictory and absurd; therefore, the Universal Doctor of the Church never taught it. Those who think that Father Descoqs didn't believe any of this himself had better think again. He was so firmly convinced of it that, if he could not persuade a friend to swallow it, he would break off the friendship. You would get your walking papers. And that would be that" (*Philosophe et théologie*, 222–223).

For quite a long time, what shocked Gilson's robust intellectual integrity more than hysterical outbursts or fanaticism was the tendency to transform Thomism into an official ideology: "Before one can call oneself a Thomist, one ought to know what the saint taught. . . . Such scruples are foreign to the most vociferous of those who wear the Thomist label. What they want is for you to call yourself a Thomist. You have to be a registered, card-carrying member of the Thomist party . . ." (Ibid., 217–218). And nothing does a more efficient job of bastardizing a philosophy. Gilson often complained about this: cf. *Les Tribulations de Sophie*, L. 9, n. 12. Nowadays, it's ancient history; but *what goes around, comes around*. It could happen again, in some other area, where all-too-human traits just such as these would be no less quick to come into play. See further, *Statuta Facultatem in Collegiis S.I. erectarum* (Statutes approved February 2, 1934), in *Acta romana S.I.* 7:615–616.

[10] Cf. É. Gilson, *Introduction à la philosophie chrétienne*, 92–93: "Augustine's cry is in everybody's memory: *Quando solidabor in Te?* It would be hard to refuse to accept as true the ontology which inspired the *Confessions*. If that isn't a real Christian philosophy and an authentic theology, there are no such things."

## 3

2, rue Collet, Vermenton (Yonne)

June 12, 1960

Étienne Gilson, of the Académie Française, with the expression of my heartfelt gratitude for the two volumes of *Exégèse médiévale*[1] that I have just found here. A simple glance reveals them to be a treasure I must wait to read until I return in ten days' time, but I'll enjoy them all the more when I get back in July.

Here is a "wicked thought", as Valéry used to say. . . . Hasn't exegesis in philosophy (I mean the exegesis of Aristotle and others) been understood, to a certain extent, by analogy with scriptural exegesis, notably by Saint Thomas Aquinas? . . . *Horrible dictu!* Although, if that's true, I'm going to have some adjusting to do, which would perhaps be *even more horrible*. . . .

Respectfully yours,

É. GILSON

[1] *Exégèse médiévale: Les quatre sens de l'Écriture*, part I, vols. 1 and 2, Théologie series, 41 (Aubier, 1959).

## 4

9, rue Saint-Romain, Paris VI$^e$

December 17, 1961

Reverend and dear Father and Colleague,

Many thanks for sending me the delightful article that I'd never have known about but for your thoughtfulness.[1] I find it excellent. In a sense, the title says it all, because it is true that man's salvation holds within itself a paradox, as you make it so admirably clear.[2] Besides, this paradox is especially so for us who, all more or less blighted by an attraction to philosophy (sometimes even—another paradox—by a need to be defenders of the Faith), willingly take man as the starting-point in our effort to reach God.[3] But Saint Thomas, as a theologian, begins with God, and there we have a miracle, but no longer a paradox. Because if God created man to raise him to eternal joy, he must have created a being (capable by nature, thus naturally capable); however, since man is a created being, he is incapable of making use of this natural ability alone and unaided. As for me, it all seems to become clear when I start from the perspective of the final cause.[4] In fact, we know by revelation that God had it in mind to save man from the moment he created him; if one admits God had this plan, one understands that he must have made intelligent creatures, capable of everything that has to do with being; and that it was possible for God, of himself, to make man capable of encountering him directly. Whence this amazing, but necessary, intellectualization: "*hoc (sc. contemplatio veritatis) tantum de operationibus humanis in Deo et in substantiis separatis est*" (*CG* III, 37). This sentence takes my breath away!

Thank you again, reverend and dear Father; have a happy Christmas, and please be sure of my appreciation and deep regard,

É. Gilson

---

[1] "Le paradoxe de l'homme ignoré des Gentils", published in *À la rencontre de Dieux; Mémorial Albert Gelin*, introd. by Maurice Jourjon and bibliography by Raymond Étaix, Bibliothèque de la faculté catholique de théologie de Lyon (Le Puy: Xavier Mappus, 1961), 8:397–414. Albert Gelin, P.S.S., 1902–1960, had been professor of Holy Scripture (Old Testament) in the department since 1937. This text, revised, would become a chapter in *Le Mystère du surnaturel* in 1965.

[2] Even the title itself must have pleased Gilson: he had

written in 1947 that the work of Saint Augustine gives us one of the most profound statements on "this fundamental paradox that constitutes the relationship of man to God" (*Philosophie et incarnation selon saint Augustin* [Montreal], 9).

[3] This criticism of method is a constant with Gilson. One may regret that his preference for a procedure more consistent with his study of Saint Thomas' thought, which proved itself to be fruitful, may have left him unaware of the technique which resulted in a contrary method, all quite correct and productive as well. Cf. L. 9.

[4] This is what he had already said in his first letter, and it is exactly in this way that I always understood it: see also L. 7, n. 4.

## 5

9, rue Saint-Roman, Paris VI<sup>e</sup>

May 13, 1962

Reverend and dear Father and Colleague,

I owe you a tremendous debt of gratitude for your book on *La Pensée religieuse du Père Teilhard de Chardin*. I took it with me to the country so I could read it in peace and quiet for a whole week; I was in dire need of a work of this kind, and I can see that among books of its type it represents a very considerable achievement, given how difficult it is to produce such a work when just the writing itself can easily lead first to scrupulosity and then to discouragement.

I knew Father Teilhard de Chardin slightly, but I never got much out of the things he wrote, which, in fact, used to be passed around in a most clandestine manner.[1] I had a really good chance to observe him on two occasions. The first time was when he baptized a baby for whom I was Godfather. It was a private baptism, at the parents' home. I have never seen a sacrament administered with more piety and priestly dignity. I shall never forget it. The second time was in New York in 1954, at the centenary (2nd?) of Columbia University. I spent three days in his company. We were participating in a philosophical-scientific colloquium: both assigned to a group presided over by the insufferable Julian Huxley. In fact, I never said a word, except to read an official communication that, in the course of the two days that followed, was never mentioned again. Sitting next to Father, I couldn't *not* take notice of his reactions. He, too, was very reserved, listening a great deal more than speaking. I couldn't help feeling that he was nonplussed by Huxley, who, however, got on his audience's nerves ("*You're very arrogant, Mr. Huxley*", a well-known Protestant theologian finally said), although Huxley's frequent appeals to evolution seemed to electrify Teilhard every time.[2]

We hadn't had much to say to each other, except, naturally, for the usual small talk. In our first encounter, though, Father dealt me a verbal one-two punch that left me reeling for three days afterward. I never regained my poise. As soon as he spotted me, he strode right up, his pleasant, handsome face lit by a smile, and clapping his hands on my shoulders, he said to me point-blank: "Hey, can you tell me if anybody's ever going to give us the scoop on this religionless Christianity we've all been waiting to hear about?" Taken aback, I spluttered a bit, finally managing to make an awkward joke of which I think the sense was that I already had enough to do to get a grip on plain Christianity, and so we left it at that. That was, as I said, in 1954. Then, I must have got embroiled in elaborate "christic" studies, since you date the essay 1955 (p. 33). To make a long story short, I shall add only that, the very same day, I saw Father sitting in an armchair, absorbed in reading his breviary and totally recollected in the midst of a busy hubbub of the crowd milling around him. I remember a rather silly thought that popped immediately into my head: when you can't wait to hear about religionless Christianity (*whatever that may be*), why in the blue blazes would you be a Jesuit? And, if you already are one, why waste time reading your breviary? I'm not saying to you that I felt all that strongly at the time, I'm just telling you what happened.

And now, to get down to brass tacks. I have asked myself a hundred times what the meaning of these terms can possibly be. Their obvious sense seems to me to be that Christ has always been and still is the cutting edge of a cosmic evolution, of a religiosity which must sooner or later either pass away or replace itself with something entirely different. I'll take any meaning you give me, but if "métachristianisme" means anything at all, it means that Christianity is something that must disappear. On opening your book, I promised myself that I would search through it with special care to see if I could find anything which would clarify the meaning of these words of Father's. I soon found, p. 89, an excellent page on his use of super-, hyper-, and even neo-, in regard to his language "in a latter period"; you can now, officially, add meta- to your list, and, of course, I assure you, I am not arguing with your commentary in the least; it's just that I have no idea of how to apply it to the words that were said to me, words I'll never forget, because they were such a shock to me. It's pretty hard to define what you mean by a "Super-Christ",[3] because if all you mean is a revelation, or a discovery that Christ is always becoming greater in our eyes, it then becomes a question of a Christian super-revelation, not of a Super-Christ (Überchristus). But if it is a "métachristianisme", a Christianity which has gone beyond religion and beyond its very self, then it must be Christianity itself, and not just *our* Christianity, which by this definition has to be surpassed. *Christus semper major* . . . , what's that, some nifty new Ignatian slogan? Seriously—I'm not just being a smart-aleck, but I would much more easily understand *semper ad majorem Christi gloriam*, and as for any expression containing a "*super-Christum*", a "*hyper-Christum*", or a "*meta-Christum*", I have trouble seeing how they even can *sound* Christian. Never mind "christogenesis" (p. 91). I can't imagine how he flatters himself in believing that he is "making Christ greater than anything" by inviting us to go beyond him. I am not going to draw any conclusion from all this except to say, as Maurice Blondel whom you quote on the same page did, that God hasn't given me the grace to understand these things, and that makes it my duty to have nothing to say about them. My only fear is that the Holy Office may find itself obliged to do quite the opposite. And it won't be attacks against doctrine that will bring about the condemnation of Teilhard's works; not by a long shot. It will be the defenses written in his favor that will inevitably get his books placed on the Index.[4] If it doesn't happen, that will be a sure sign that Father's religionless Christianity has already come to pass. I dare say he didn't consider himself its John the Baptist, but at least John the Baptist's Christ was "the Christ of the Gospel". I wouldn't want to upset you by asking the same question he asked himself, to which he was well-equipped to find the answer; yet, he evaded it after all. Your whole paragraph on page 92, "Finally, then, let us make no mistake about it . . .", fine as it is, leaves me completely unconvinced. I can't get rid of the mental image of my neighbor in 1954, whom the word "evolution" snapped to attention every time he heard it, the same way a priest in choir doffs his biretta at the name of Jesus. I don't doubt for a second that he died in the love of Christ; here, it's a matter of discussing thought and knowledge, not whether he loved the Christ of the Gospel—there can be no further question of that—but what I want to know is what he thought of Christ. I never did understand Teilhard; even after having read him I still don't, and maybe you don't understand him too well yourself. If, by chance, this might be the case, at least please be assured that in that respect, I understand *you* perfectly.

I thank you with all my heart for this nice book, and please accept, reverend and dear Father and colleague, my warmest good wishes and best regards,

É. GILSON

[1] These words seem to show conclusively that Gilson never really read Teilhard. There is no evidence, to my knowledge, that he ever read anything but a few of his essays, and always with a bias against Teilhard. He was put off by several formulae—more especially the one he heard in 1954 at the colloquium at Columbia University, an expression that he interpreted with the strictest logical and metaphysical rigor, and from these formulae that shocked him, he understood, or rather imagined, what Teilhard's thought was all about. In fact, Teilhard customarily sent his books to the Father-General in Rome, or to the Provincial at Lyon, for approval. Gilson didn't know that.

[2] Gilson must have transferred to Teilhard some of the

annoyance that "the insufferable Julian Huxley" provoked in himself. In reality, far from being "electrified" by the lecturer, if Teilhard took a lively interest in what Huxley had to say, it was more probably because he himself was at that time in the act of bringing out a "little book on Man" in which he was trying to "'correct' the sometimes dangerous views" recently proposed by Huxley in *The Future of Man*; particularly his agnosticism and his "neohumanism" which he considered utopian, and it bothered Teilhard that Huxley did not know how to offer a purpose to human action and that he mixed human evolution up with progress toward a golden age. The truth is, that at this international meeting on "the unity of human knowledge", where there were about seventy participants, a gulf opened between "scientists" and "humanists", and Teilhard deplored the fact that the few Christians present (Gilson for the Catholics and Niebuhr for the Protestants were both opposed to innovation, "immobilists") had no strategic position from which to counter a more or less atheistic evolutionism. Later *L'Énergie d'évolution* (1953), and also *Les Singularités de l'espèce humaine* (posthumously published, 1955) criticized Huxley's *Evolutionary Humanism* and *Humanism in Action* (as well as G. Simpson, Charles Galton-Darwin, and J. Rostand). Cf. Teilhard de Chardin, *Lettres intimes* (Aubier 1974), 443–447.

[3]Cf. H. de Lubac, *La Pensée religieuse du Père Pierre Teilhard de Chardin* (Aubier, 1962), 89–92. The "commentary" I owe in large part to Teilhard himself: "By 'Super-Christ', I absolutely do not mean another Christ, . . . different from the original and greater than he; rather I mean the same Christ, the Christ who always has been, revealing himself to us in larger, renewed . . . form and dimensions . . ."; p. 272: "Christianity remains completely consistent with itself . . ."; moreover, "*Christus semper major*" was a loan translation derived from "*Deus semper major*" and had nothing to do with Teilhard. Gilson was not, by the way, wrong to find fault

with the simplistic expressions and catch-phrases that Teilhard, far from his home, ill, and grown old, used so lavishly toward the end without always making himself clear, buzzwords that hid a system of thought much more deeply rooted in Catholic tradition than people often were willing to believe.

[4] Better informed in the larger context, Father Janssens, Father-General of the Society, wrote to me on August 27, 1962: "In my judgment, your book was helpful to the Church and served the cause of truth, and I wanted it to be published. I don't regret my decision." And it is a fact that neither Pius XII, nor John XXIII, nor Paul VI gave in to the pressures that were put on them in that regard; quite the opposite. I said something about this in *Teilhard posthume* (Fayard, 1977), 133–147. Cf. L. 9 and 10.

6

Institute of Mediaeval Studies
Queen's Park
Toronto, Ont., Canada

April 1, 1964

Reverend and dear Father and Colleague,

I was blessed, literally, to be able to state publicly
the high regard in which I hold you and your
work.[1] I've never read anything of yours without
sensing an atmosphere of friendliness. I think
minds behave like cats: they sniff noses for a second and know immediately if God has disposed
them to friendship or to enmity. I had another
occasion to note our comradeship recently at
Montreal. I spent a week with the Dominican
Fathers, giving four lectures on *The Spirit of
Thomism*. The second one had to do with "the
master-plan of Creation" (a title I considered a bit
exaggerated for publicity's sake), and in that lecture I planned to reread passages from *Surnaturel*.[2]
I could only say you were right, because what
you say is true. *No doubt is possible on this subject.*[3]

I'm going to say the same thing again in two weeks' time at the 175th centenary [*sic*] of Georgetown University, S.J., in Washington. I don't think it will provoke a scandal. As a theologian you're tops, but you are also a humanist in the great tradition of humanist theologians. The latter don't care much for the Scholastics and the Scholastics generally detest them. Why? It's partly, I suppose, because Scholastics understand only propositions that are simple and unequivocal, or which seem so to be. You humanists are more interested in the truth the formula is intended to state, some of which always escapes and will not be imprisoned within the proposition.[4] When the Scholastics don't comprehend it any more, they get nervous, and since they can't be sure that what is eluding them isn't false, they condemn the principle because it's *safer*. Your priceless pearl brings me to my point.[5] In my third lecture for Georgetown, I have written the following:

Thomas Aquinas was not a particularly safe Thomist; rather than safe, he preferred to be right, which is not the same thing. The safe Thomist prefers not to say the whole truth if to assert it unqualifiedly risks misleading his readers. Thomas proceeds differently. Having first made sure of the truth, he states it as forcibly as possible; after all, if his

68

meaning is clear, those who misinterpret it are responsible for their own errors.[6]

Your theologian's ghastly comment is a perfect witness to the indifference of so many pious souls to the meaning of the word truth. That's the way Father Boyer is[7] (I don't like everybody). The most extraordinary phenomenon I've seen yet in this sense is *Doctor communis*.[8] The cheek of exchanging a *Doctor communis* for the Universal Doctor is the last straw. When I quote them Saint Thomas on the Faith, they accuse me of fideism. No! Not of fideism, but of "leaning dangerously toward fideism".[9] I never dignify that with an answer. My great strength, alas! is that I am not a priest. Had Maritain and I been monks or priests, neither of us would have been able to write the hundredth part of what we've written.[10] We'd have been, as they say here, *crucified*. But I've nothing to teach you on that score, have I? Nonetheless, there will have to be a new edition of *Surnaturel*.[11]

It's snowing here today and I'm thinking of you in that marvelous town of Aix, near Pernes-les-Fontaines, where people really understand the art of living.[12] I'm happy you're there. Please don't worry any more than you have to about the opinions of those who don't know how to think. I know they do some harm, but as I once said to a monk-friend of mine: it would be only too lovely to be a monk, if only the Church didn't take it upon herself to make you do a little penance for the privilege. Say hello for me to the Trois-Dauphins fountain[13] and please accept my warmest personal regards.

Respectfully,

É. GILSON

[1] I can't remember any more what public token of esteem it was for which I had thanked Gilson.

[2] He had alluded to this book previously on July 8, 1956, and December 17, 1961 (L. 1 and 4). However, he does not seem to have given it a close reading before 1964. Cf. L. 8 (June 20, 1965): "How could I have remained insensitive to the entire first part of the old edition of *Surnaturel*? . . .": and also the beginning, perhaps a little romanticized, of his article from *La Croix* (Appendix II).

[3] Gilson would restate his agreement to me several times, from the triple standpoint of history, doctrinal truth, and the "centrality" of the problem. Cf. L. 7, 8, and 9 (June 1965); already L. 1 (July 1956), 2 (May 1960), and 3 (December 1961). On June 19 and 20, 1965, he would commend me in Saint Thomas' name for having refused to admit that in regard to the "beatific vision" man is in a state of *potentia obedientiae tantum*. What he also liked in *Surnaturel* was the synthesis of Saint Augustine and Saint Thomas (L. 2, May 21, 1960); a theme on which he would enlarge on June 21, 1965 (L. 9), and in the article in *La Croix*.

*Le Mystère du Surnaturel* has brought me, ever since 1946,

the most contradictory reviews imaginable. I shall quote only two. The severity of the second will excuse me for publishing the extravagance of the first.

a) From New York, where he had found refuge from Hitler's persecution after a brief stay in France, the celebrated professor Dietrich von Hildebrand wrote to me in 1949, "*Sancti Hilarii Ep. Conf. Ecclesiae doctoris*": "I have been planning to write to you for a long time. I have read and studied your great work, *Surnaturel*, in depth and I can't tell you how much insight and intellectual profit I gained from reading it. It is one of the greatest theological achievements of modern times, and besides its immense erudition and the power of its arguments, its conclusion is one of breathtaking beauty, profundity, and truth. I can't express the importance I attach to your fresh articulation of basic truth, your return to the sources, and the quality of light you throw on so many other problems by means of this very sound book. I was especially thrilled by your study of humility in the chapter 'the prayer of Adam'."

b) *Gethsémani. Réflexions sur le mouvement théologique contemporain*, by Cardinal Joseph Siri (Téqui, 1981; 2nd ed., a completion of the French translation of a work first published in Rome, *Fraternité de la Trés Sainte Vierge Marie*):

". . . In 1946 he published his book *Surnaturel*. . . . He affirmed that the supernatural order is not without basis because it is indebted to nature. Thus, if one leaves aside the gratuitousness of the supernatural order, nature by the very fact of its existence is identified with the supernatural. . . . The fundamental reasoning can be expressed in this fashion: the act of reasoning intellectually carries within itself the possibility of consulting the notion of the infinite; this is why the supernatural is implied in human nature in itself. This vision of the intimate and essential reality of man was foreshadowed in the previous writings of Father de Lubac. . . . His speculative argument is constructed as something apart from the principles, apart from the notions hitherto accepted as basic principles of the Faith, etc. This non-gratuitousness of the supernatural order . . . leads easily to a kind of cosmic monism, to an anthropocentric idealism" (pp. 57–62). Cardinal Siri did me the honor of being the first of a trio (the other two being Karl Rahner and Jacques Maritain) who brought about a revival of modernism "with a new vocabulary and new subtleties of expression", embodying "the effect of Revelation replaced by an expanded 'religious sense' in the subconscious", and pressing "almost beyond its origin toward a quasi-'transcendental' agnosticism and a 'dogmatic evolutionism', so as to destroy all aspects of objectivity in Revelation and in acquired knowledge" (pp. 51–52). Since then, a propaganda-system has surrounded and taken advantage of this work and the ones that came after it, in such a way that, by means of a cascade of intricate genealogies, I am becoming the heir of Feuerbach and the ancestor of the "liberation theologians".

[4] What he liked about me (as he told me) was a certain "humanism" which had something in common with his own much richer, vaster and (if I may say so) more fertile humanism; a certain feeling for analogy and mystery, a real independence from the word-webs of the Schools and from arguments drawn from illegitimate authorities ("John of Saint Thomas teaches . . ."), qualities that, he believed, kept me close to the spirit of Saint Thomas. Cf. L. 8 and 9 (June 20 and 21, 1965), and L. 12 (May 16, 1967). Father Gerald Smith, who was a close friend of his, wrote me about him on December 31, 1960: "Gilson knows the score, . . ." (see Appendix III; L. 2 and 3).

His humanism, which characterizes all his work, has borne fruit in at least a dozen volumes, published at different times. Notable, for example, is his lively interest in Erasmus, who, in his view, should have much to bring to our era because he recognized that theology and philosophy are interdependent, that all forms of "modernism" are either errors or

72

outright lies, and that despite exterior alterations the Church is indestructible; one of his Toronto lectures of 1964 analyzed the dispute with Luther: "The Fly and the Elephant". His "Rabelais franciscain", published in the first issue of the *Revue d'histoire franciscaine* (begun in 1924 by his friend Henri Lemaître), in which he criticized the teaching of Abel Lefranc at the Collège de France, is an indictment of the then-current idea (which resurfaces from time to time) that all the great Renaissance humanists had forsaken medieval Christianity to pave the way for modern unbelief (cf. Shook, *Gilson*, 130–131, 236, 368–369). See his book *Les Idées et les lettres* (1932; 2nd ed., 1955), *Dante et la philosophie* (1939), *Héloïse et Abélard*, 2nd ed. (1948), etc. By exploring several salient points in the thought of Pico della Mirandola, Charles de Bouelles, and Erasmus, I found myself paddling along in Gilson's wake.

[5] I had quoted to him a reply I overheard at the end of a meeting of the Commission on Doctrine at the Council: "*Haec quae dixit Excellentia vestra sunt quidem verissima, sed prorsus periculosa.*" [What you said, Your Excellency, is all too true, but certainly dangerous.]

[6] Cf. Appendix III, 2.3 and L. 3. It was in April 1964 that Gilson gave his Georgetown Lectures on *The Spirit of Thomism* (New York, 1964).

[7] Father Charles Boyer, who was no dunce, and whom Gilson correctly cast in the role of "brilliant second" to Father Garrigou-Lagrange, became for him later on the spokesman for this decadent, conventional, and authoritarian form of "Thomism", the mechanism of which Gilson analyzes in the long letter of June 21, 1965 (L. 9), giving several examples. (But the words quoted were not Father Boyer's.) Gilson, however, did Father Boyer justice in his historical study on *La Formation de saint Augustin* (Beauchesne, 1920) refuting the "diametrically opposed" viewpoint of Prosper Alfaric (*L'Évolution intellectuelle de saint Augustin* [Nourry, 1918]),

by clarifying the importance of examining carefully the arguments put forward by Alfaric, *God and Philosophy*, 2nd ed., (1960), 44, note.

[8] An allusion to the Roman publication of this name, whose Scholastic "philosophism" and "low-grade rationalism" struck him as being contrary to the doctrine and spirit of the real "Universal Doctor".

[9] In his L. 1, Gilson had cited the case, similar to his own, of Father Sertillanges, who had been accused of agnostic leanings just the way he had been accused of leaning toward fideism.

[10] Gilson had been acutely pained by the placing on the Index of the little book by Father M. D. Chenu, O.P., on the theological school of Saulchoir (1943). Cf. his letter to Pegis, April 1, 1947:

> The situation of Father M. D. Chenu is still deteriorating, nobody knows why, except that three French Canadian bishops have raised objections to his teaching in Montreal or, *a fortiori*, Quebec. . . . It is a great pity and my heart is bleeding for my friend. . . . He is in just the situation where Maritain and I would be, were we priests. God seems to be saving a few laymen to very definitive purposes. Let this be off the record" (Shook, *Gilson*, 276).

He had been no less affected by the machinations of a "Scholasticist" cabal who had tried to obtain other condemnations and who, partially disappointed or even angered by the encyclical *Humani generis* (1950), had put out some incorrect interpretations of it based on their own assumptions. This is what he demonstrated in Rome in September 1950, at the International Thomist Congress, and then in December, in Milwaukee, at a conference at Marquette University. Cf. L. 2, 16, n. 4, and Appendix III, L. 3.

[11] I had envisaged a new edition in 1949, for which I had

74

written a prefatory note: ". . . Among the numerous studies this book has occasioned or that have dealt, since it was published, with kindred subjects, there have been a goodly number of really positive advances. . . . M. Gilson's recent book on *L'Être et l'Essence* (1948), by explaining the evolution of traditional philosophy in the West, could not fail to make possible a better understanding of the parallel evolution of theology. Similarly full of information is the debate begun by Father Gerald Smith, S.J., and Mr. Anton G. Pegis, president of the Pontifical Institute of Mediaeval Studies in Toronto, at the Congress of American Catholic Philosophers held in Boston in April 1949. . . ." Although *Surnaturel* has not been reprinted, the essentials of it have been restated, without change in basic purpose, in two works. The first section, enlarged, became in 1965 *Augustinisme et théologie moderne*. The second part and the conclusion have been re-edited in Italian, with several additions, in volume 13 of *Opera omnia*: "Spirito e Libertà" (Milan: Jaca Book), 99–270. The third part, "Aux origines du mot surnaturel", has not been redone; it could have been expanded indefinitely, but other tasks seemed more worthwhile, in my judgment. On October 18, 1957, I was able to write to my Provincial that I had received Gilson's essential approval for this book, and that, on the difference between Saint Thomas and Cajetan, a point insistently disputed by quite a few people, Gilson was willing to go much further than even I was.

[12] The letter Gilson is answering had been sent from Aix-en-Provence.

[13] Trois-Dauphins fountain is in the Saint-Jean-de-Malte section of the city.

## 7

June 19, 1965

Reverend and dear Father and Friend,

The postman just brought me your two latest books at the moment when I was leaving Paris for Vermenton (Yonne). Faced with having to leave one of them behind, I am reluctantly putting aside *Augustinisme et théologie*, which I will take up and read upon my return, but I am furiously shoving the other one[1] into my bag and I'm impatient to get my teeth into it. First of all, thank you for having given me a place of honor in it. It's not just the honor that pleases me, it's your friendship. Yes, thank you very much indeed! You are right to insist on the natural vocation of the intellect to a vision of God of which it is naturally incapable. Your Thomistic texts are conclusive,[2] but I don't even know whether people are conscious of the centrality of the problem.[3] I recently heard an eminent Dominican theologian publicly state his admiration for the notion of potentiality subject to obedience, so appropriate for settling the argument. But I don't believe Saint Thomas ever spoke of potentiality subject to obedience in this context. The beatific vision is *supernatural*, but it isn't a *miracle*![4] Of course, I'm carrying coals to Newcastle, telling this to you!

Thank you again, and please be sure of my sincere respect and best regards,[5]

É. GILSON

[1]*Le Mystère du surnaturel*. This work, which amplified a 1949 article, was dedicated to Father Gerald Smith, S.J. The reason will be seen in Appendix III, Smith's L. 5. The "place of honor" accorded to Gilson, was the text placed in evidence: "Buried under five centuries of deposits, ignorance of itself is the most serious ill from which Scholasticism is suffering. To cure it, let us listen to the counsel of history: Return to theology!" (É. Gilson, "Les recherches historico–critiques et l'avenir de la Scholastique", in *Scholastica ratione historico-critica instauranda* [Rome, 1951], 142.)

[2]An important theologian had, however, written to me: "If you can establish the opposite thesis (to the one the Thomists hold), affirmed in *Surnaturel* without a shred of proof, no one will be more grateful to you than I, whose only wish . . . is to know the authentic thought of Saint Thomas. . . . While contradicting the interpretation shared by theologians and historians on this point [the natural love of God] as on so many other questions, you don't feel the need to bolster your claims by any sort of evidence, doubtless because you are used to being taken at your word by your students. . . . You really must learn that we are not pupils

77

waiting for their professor to be kind enough to write a grade in the margin of their paper." The author contrasted my "methods" with "the ones that eminent teachers in historical sciences whose courses I had been privileged to take . . . had taught me" and listed among them M. Gilson.

[3] By means of this double publication in 1965, which pleased Gilson so much, I was not just trying to clarify still more and to provide a better justification for an ancient philosophical tradition that modern Scholasticism had done a lot to blot out. But, as I explained in a preface to *Le Mystère du surnaturel* (pp. 13–17), after having exhausted, in a violent rear-guard action, the last of its usefulness in the Schools, this "dualist", or rather separatist theory now ran the risk, with the unthinking participation of its surviving defenders, of producing its most bitter fruit. Around 1950, I was rather well placed to observe this, and as a result I felt personally obligated to keep up the effort I had long since undertaken, especially since I had been encouraged to do so. My fears were not groundless: as what followed showed all too well. The wave of secularism, to which certain guardians of orthodoxy had turned a blind eye, was already rolling into the innermost preserves of the Church. Seeing what was coming, I tried to rally people one last time, by making as clear as I could, "the basic truth, which must never be allowed to be obscured or corrupted".

[4] This reference to "potentiality subject to obedience" came from a state of confusion, current at the time among Thomists of every school. Cf. J. Maritain, speaking of the "Thomist theologians" in *Distinguer pour unir* (1935 edition), 422: in relation to "God seen clearly, as a completely supernatural object, created intelligence is nothing but potentiality subject to obedience." Here Gilson is not merely expressing himself advisedly as a historian; in a few words, he strikes at the root of the problem. He will say again, in his *Constantes philosophiques de l'être*, 230: "The deepest secret of Christian

philosophy is perhaps the relationship, at once simple and incomprehensible, that it dares to set up between nature and the supernatural end for which nature was created, even though it may be impossible for nature naturally to have an inkling of its own existence and even though nature naturally has no right to expect even that much." It will be noticed how this accords with H. Urs von Balthasar, "Petite memoire sur Paul Claudel", *Bulletin de la Société Paul Claudel* 81:73: "Thomas Aquinas sees man as one whose duty it is to think about being in a precise balance between nature and supernature; because by nature man is called to revelation as a gift of God, and although he has no right to this revelation, he is incapable of reaching his final end without it. . . ." Cf. H. de Lubac, *Surnaturel* (1946), 135–139, etc.

On the basis of the interpretation of Saint Thomas given by R. Garrigou-Lagrange, Maria Ritz, in her thesis at Fribourg, Switzerland, on "the problem of being in Maurice Blondel's ontology" (1958), would criticize (albeit moderately) Blondel's thought. See the characteristic sentence from Garrigou-Lagrange's *De Revelatione*, 3rd ed., 96–97, cited as an example on page 96 of the thesis, etc.

[5] This letter and the two that followed it, dated on three successive days, seem to me worthwhile for their picturesque spontaneity as well as for their doctrinal interest. In this one, the allusion to the "centrality of the problem" which many intellectuals in the Church really seemed to know nothing about (except that they were against it), is remarkable.

## 8

6, Rue Collet, Vermenton, Yonne

June 20, 1965

Reverend and dear Father, Colleague, and Friend,

A belated, but providential, inspiration made me add the first volume to my baggage at the last minute. All I've done is read it—all the way from Paris to Vermenton and, once I got here, all the rest of the day and a good part of the night. How could I have remained insensitive to the whole first part of the old edition of *Surnaturel*? In the first place, I've never had a copy of my own, and it's been out of print; then, too, I can't stand Baius, so I must have skipped over the section on him at the beginning of the book; he put me off (he'll put others off too and I'm not sure that he should be right at the beginning);[1] finally and above all, my abysmal ignorance of post-medieval theology, which causes me untold misery (I've never even *seen* a volume of Soto),[2] makes it hard for me to follow a guide, even one as wise and careful as you, through such extremely subtle arguments.

It is like trying to describe, with the help of a guidebook, a country one has never visited.[3]

This time, I think I've almost got it, and I owe you my deepest gratitude for that.[4] Volume II, I'll bet, will be easy for me, since I've already looked at it before. I agree completely with you on the root of the problem. Besides, you call my attention to some texts I didn't know about, or whose importance I perhaps missed when I first read *Surnaturel* (in the well-thumbed copy belonging to the Montreal Dominicans). I would have given you credit and used them if I'd known about them when I wrote the little essay you were kind enough to quote. The short quotation from Saint Thomas, III, 9, 2, which I considered conclusive, was already in your book, p. 243, note 4.[5] I don't think either of us has ever found a set of terms adequate to define the Thomist position, and that's quite to be expected, since he himself could not find one either. In fact, his terminology is somewhat loose, because he never throws away an expression if it is possible to justify it *in some sense*. Potentiality subject to obedience is an instructive example of what I'm talking about. He came upon the term ready-made; strictly speaking, it is applicable only to miracles, where nothing in matter either prepares for, expects, or makes the phenomenon possible; in general (your excellent quotes on page 244), all nature is in a state of potentiality subject to obedience to whatever it may please

God to do with it, provided that this is not, in itself, contradictory or impossible. You are right to say that in the case of the beatific vision, one could not say that the human soul might be, in that respect, in a state of *potentiality subject to obedience*, but I don't know of a text where it would be expressed that way, nor even whether he spoke of *potentiality subject to obedience* in this context anyhow. Why? Because all he was trying to do was to make it clear that the word *obedience* is a poor way of expressing the relationship of nature to grace. A creature made in the image of God doesn't have to "obey" to want to grow in likeness to its model; no doubt it is obedient, but it obeys the same way we obey an order that coincides exactly with our own dearest wish. Nobody will ever be able to capture, in a phrase, the synchronous, but not identically-related, natural and supernatural character of this natural desire to see God.[6]

An ex-Benedictine, J. Laporta[7] (131, Avenue Général-Médecin-Derache, Brussels—5), married, father of a family, dumped an enormous manuscript on my doorstep about two years ago. I didn't understand much of it then, but now I wonder whether I might not have happened upon a species of Baïanism. It's something I know nothing about. I made him cut his manuscript considerably; I made him take out a lot of critical comments I felt were superfluous (he still had a lot left, and maybe you were the target of some of them), but what he wanted to prove is that the beatific vision *is not* a case of potentiality subject to obedience. Very well; even now I don't know if I succeeded or failed in helping him explain that it was, or indeed wasn't, a case of *potentiality subject to nature*. I'm going to keep his book in my collection, guessing that perhaps he lost his vocation and his faith under pressure from orthodox judges who wanted to make him confess that the beatific vision is, *primo et per se*, a case of potentiality subject to obedience. . . . But I'm afraid I encountered the opposite error as far as he was concerned. You'll see. . . .

I've just done something really dumb. I sent an article to *France catholique* protesting the new French translation which obliges us to sing, in the *Credo*, that the Son is of the *same nature* as the Father. I maintain that they have been consubstantial from eternity, and that this is not exactly the same thing.[8] I hope Jean de Fabrègues will throw the article in the wastebasket.[9]

Respectfully and affectionately yours,

É. GILSON

[1] Gilson, no doubt, was right. The placement of the chapters on Baius and Jansen at the beginning of the book was due to circumstances beyond my control, and so accidental that I just didn't think of a better arrangement at the time: first, I had made a thorough study of these two authors in 1930 in the old library of the Collège Saint-Joseph (Lyon, rue Sainte-Hélène), well-stocked with sixteenth- and seventeenth-century authors; then, Father d'Alès, secretary of *Recherches de science religieuse*, had edited the pages I had compiled on these two authors in a terrible hurry.

[2] On Dominic de Soto (1494–1560), O.P., who participated in the Council of Trent: biographical note by V. Bertrand de Heredia, *Dictionnaire de théologie catholique*, vol. 14: cols. 2423–2431.

[3] Gilson's "ignorance" on this period was not as serious as he thought it was; anyway, he had understood what was essential in his analysis of Cajetan: the celebrated commentator on the *Summa Theologiae* opened the door to systems Thomistic and otherwise in modern Scholasticism. "Cajetan's point of departure depends on this fundamental axiom: '*Natura non largitur inclinationem ad aliquid, ad quod tota vis naturae perducere nequit.*'" J. Laporta, in the work cited below, with different references.

One writer that I think Gilson has, however, neglected, is Denys the Carthusian. It is particularly instructive to compare this author with Cajetan. Denys (along with several others), toward the end of the fifteenth century, already essentially holds the modern thesis, but only in order to use it for the express purpose of opposing Saint Thomas', which he undertakes to refute point by point—whereas, at the beginning of the sixteenth century, Cajetan pretends to be commenting on Saint Thomas'. See the texts and references in *Augustinisme* and in *Le Mystère du surnaturel*.

[4] Cf. L. 6, n. 1.

[5] There must have been a mistake in the reference given

by Gilson. See, rather, *Prima Secundae*, q. 113, a. 10, or q. 6, a. 5, ad 2.

[6]Behind the correctness of these explanations, one will note the good sense and intellectual modesty that inspire them.

[7]J. Laporta, *Pour trouver le sens exact des termes "appetitus naturalis", "desiderium naturale", "amor naturalis", etc., chez Thomas d'Aquin*: "Introduction. For four centuries people have been discussing the doctrine of Thomas Aquinas on the destiny of human nature. The origin of this controversy can be traced to Cajetan's interpretation of the term 'natural desire'. In the famous text of the *Summa Theologiae* 1ᵃ 2ᵃᵉ, q. 3, a. 8, c, Thomas explains that the natural desire, on the part of the intellectual, to know, can find rest only by attaining the sight of the divine essence."

(This curious term "the intellectual" is out of place in French; likewise, p. 61, "The natural end in no way brings to fulfillment the blossoming of an intellectual. . . ." For Saint Thomas, it is a matter of the intellectual being, that is, the spiritual being, be it man or angel, who for him is basically defined by its intelligence. Finally, p. 95, the author says it a bit better: "The purpose of grace and glory is nothing but to fulfill the deepest natural desire of every intellectual being.")

" 'This natural desire to see God', Cajetan comments, 'is the conscious need, arising "naturally" in man, once he has been instructed by revelation that he is in fact called to this supernatural blessedness'. Cajetan's error is to consider the natural desire for the beatific vision as a psychological activity. And many modern commentators, even if they throw out Cajetan's interpretation, still remain attached to this basic mistake of seeing in the natural appetite for the sight of God a conscious desire of the will. For Thomas the natural appetite is the finality of a being. All of nature tends toward its end, 'desires' it 'naturally'. . . . With Thomas, it is never a question of a conscious desire of the will that would 'naturally' arise in man at the news of his supernatural calling. It is by the supernatural virtues of faith, hope, and love that man freely pursues the beatific vision when he has learned by revelation that God in fact is calling him to it . . ." (pp. 37–39). *Archives d'histoire doctrinale et littéraire du Moyen Age*, année 1973 (Vrin, 1974), 37–95. (Cf. likewise, "Les notions d'appétit naturel et de puissance obédientielle chez saint Thomas", in *Ephemerides theologiae lovanienses* 5, 2 [1928].)

When Father Laberthonnière, having grasped the necessity of clarifying the idea of supernatural and of changing the definitions which had become prevalent in modern Scholasticism, wrote in 1901: "The manner of describing the supernatural . . . leaves room for all kinds of mixups and misunderstandings", and when he said again in 1931, in a letter to D. Parodi: "What I hold against the theologians . . ., is that they have required as a matter of faith that all of us be 'potentialities subject to obedience'", *in that much* he, an Augustinian, was a better Thomist than a lot of modern Scholastics, Thomists, and Suarezians all together.

[8] That is undeniable, and since it is a matter of the very core of the Christian Faith, Gilson's agitation is understandable, as is that of many others. The expression "of the same nature" certainly does not deny the "consubstantial", so one can say that the Faith is safe; but it does not express it concisely either; it does not offer an exact equivalent to "consubstantial". It is especially regrettable in this regard, that the liturgical translations were made, and then officially adopted, sometimes in too hasty a fashion, without sufficient safeguards. Two years later, in *Les Tribulations de Sophie*, Gilson will mention his disappointment with the all-too-numerous liturgical jumbles, poorly explained to the faithful and sometimes introduced in a disorderly and whimsical way: "Putting the sixteen documents of Vatican II into practice has had a concrete result whose consequence is, tangibly, a

disruption in ritual rather more disconcerting to the faithful than the diocesan or parochial reformers ever foresaw." He will also deplore the disappearance of certain particularly beautiful texts: "Some of the loveliest parts of the Liturgy are, in this way, slipping little by little into oblivion: '*Deus qui humanae substantiae dignitatem mirabiliter condidisti et mirabilius reformasti*', . . . who knows that sublime prayer any more? . . ." (pp. 162, 163). But with him, it was never a question of objecting in principle to the liturgical reform wrought by the Council. Not at all. He recognized the action of a Church that "must be all things to all men" and to which no taste for antiquity, no reluctance to change long-standing habits, no faulty understanding of tradition has any right to create obstacles. He even gives rather short shrift to those who, trying to find "a proper aesthetic purpose in worship", consequently wished to retain or to introduce "an essentially impure factor into the pursuit of its proper end, which is basically religious". He knows besides that any "updating of the Church" inevitably occasions misunderstandings and hindrances that it has to know how to rise above, and he accepts in all simplicity that "each time a reform is effected, a generation may be sacrificed to that improvement." As for the change from Latin into modern languages, he supports without a second thought the reasons that Paul VI gave for this many times, and he does not insist upon perfect translations, because he knows very well that "no perfect translation is possible." Concerning the liturgical texts themselves, the implementation of the Council's directives was a more delicate matter, since what was being laid aside was not a language the Church had borrowed long ago, but a tongue she herself had created for the proper expression of her Faith, and that was the mother tongue of the Christian West. "It's all right about the changes in form", Gilson admits, not wishing to be thought a quibbler or a trafficker in nostalgia, but don't let changes in form bring on "any loss in substance"! Yet,

87

this is what seemed to him to be happening, in French, in the "translation" of the "*consubstantialem Patri*", taken from the Council of Nicaea. In chapter 4 of his short work on *La Société de masse et sa culture*, (Vrin, 1967), "Liturgies de masse", he will explain his views on this at greater length and, in my opinion, much more astutely. He cites the two examples of Italy and the United States, whose translations are correct, simple, and effortless. On the egregious French translation, he says with a tinge of irony, "it's hard to imagine that the French translation would have been kept for an instant without good and serious reasons, but since no one has said what those reasons are, the mind of the ordinary believer can only boggle at what is happening. They probably thought the faithful wouldn't ask questions. That was a psychological error. New forms of prayer can't be imposed on believers brought up in the conviction that the substance of dogma is intangible without giving them a bit of a shock. . . . If the Son is of the same nature as the Father, he is God like him, but if he isn't of the same substance or the same being . . ., he can be a second God, with the Holy Spirit, in the meantime, modalizing into a third. . . . As far as Judaism and Mohammedanism are concerned, Christianity is polytheism. Until now the Christian could answer no, since the three divine persons are but one and the same God; no longer can he say that, if he is French, because if the three persons have only their nature in common, not their substance or their being, each of them is a God just as the other two are. If a father and his son are two men of the same nature, the Father and the Son are two Gods".

Gilson, certainly, knew that "this isn't what they meant" (and he wisely concludes that the faithful member of the Church, be he priest or layman, who would be stubborn enough to reinsert the "consubstantial" publicly into a text that has been assigned as obligatory, would exhibit a lack of discipline). But then, he asks, "why replace the correct word

88

with one that is not? . . . Of all the priests to whom I have put this question, not one seemed to think that changing the word could be of the least importance." Undoubtedly they wanted to avoid too sophisticated a word: but in fact they replaced the utterance of a mystery with a colloquialism, thus showing a low estimation of the Christian people, and to be precise, Gilson concludes, people will have to say that "the Church of France no longer has the same Creed as the Church of Rome." It is a hard saying: however, it does not mean that the Church of France has, on any particular article of faith, a different Creed, but only that, on one fundamental article, she seems to be keeping the Faith somewhat up in the air (*La Société de masse*, 116–131). Cf. L. 13, n. 1.

[9]He had chosen a rather provocative title: "Am I a Schismatic?" ["Suis-je schismatique?"], not suspecting that it might be used against him. On June 29, before it was published, he joked about it in a letter to his friend Shook: ". . . I am in the act of making . . . a new schism, that of stone-age Nicaean Catholics who believe that the Son is of the same 'substance' as the Father. . . . In short, I'm asking our liturgical authorities to put the old '*consubstantialem Patri*' back into the Creed. Everyone warns me that I'm going to provoke an 'outcry': the notion of substance is not acceptable in the modern mentality." Fabrègues printed the article, which raised a stir. In a second letter to Shook, on July 11, Gilson evidences surprise and no little distress at the number of people who either took seriously, or acted as though they took seriously, his interrogative title's reference to schism: "It was a purely rhetorical question." Others, less prone to muddy the issue, nevertheless were sorry he had made his objection in the public press. But some good souls told him they agreed with him, and some requests for revision were sent to the official translators. The translators, judging that Arianism is no longer a danger in this day and age, refused to pay any attention. Notwithstanding, one of the theologians

who had alerted them observed, it remains "necessary to express the Faith correctly". The net result of this commotion was that the faithful Gilson felt "marginalized". This seeming indifference to the meet and right enunciation of the Faith hurt him quite a bit. As late as July 17, 1966, he wrote to his friend Pegis:

> I am now considered retrograde because 'nature' is left-ist whereas 'substance' is rightist. . . . These modern liturgists are so naïve that they find 'nature' easier to understand than 'substance'. By Jove, if they ever succeed in making the dogma of the Trinity even slightly intelligible, they will have done a remarkable thing (In Shook, *Gilson*, 371).

## 9

6, rue Collet, Vermenton, Yonne

June 21, 1965

Reverend and dear Father and Friend,

*Le Mystère du surnaturel*, which I have just thor-
oughly enjoyed reading from cover to cover, is
absolutely perfect.[1] I really have the impression,
not that the question is closed, because people
always have to muddle things up, but that it ought
to be. You've said all that can be said, particularly
the very important counsel that eventually there
comes a time when one must be silent. It truly is
a mystery that is at issue here. As for your pages
179–183, I was just about to say that not only are
they cast in the mold of the most reliable Thomistic thought, but they include, which is so important, Saint Thomas' manner of speaking.[2] Others
(those who are not of the ilk of masters like
Augustine and Bonaventure, for example) take
theology as their object, while Thomas, Augustine, and all the great ones, take for their goal the
One theology is all about, created reality seen in

the light of divine revelation, and God himself before everything else. This is why every theology worthy of the name ends by stopping itself, not short, but stumbling and bumbling before the essential ineffability of God. Saint Thomas possessed this sense of mystery in the highest degree, but since he was, at the same time, imbued with boundless admiration for the intellect—for the two great wonders are that there can be both being and knowledge—he often sets us to grappling with positions that consist in defining exactly the intelligible shape of a mystery whose complete philosophical elucidation is impossible.

It seems to me that Cajetan is done for. Very soon we'll be called upon to stand up for him, and you've already started. I'm fully aware that sometimes I overdo it, but after due reflection and in all objectivity, I think I would still label it a *corruptorium*.[3] For two reasons. His commentary on the *first* article of the *Summa Theologiae* topples the whole book off the track from the very outset; then, representing himself as interpreting the meaning of the work, he proceeds to lead Saint Thomas' readers astray. It took me years to figure that out. When I finally did, and said something about it, I was afraid it would be a shock to everyone; I was astonished that I got no reaction at all. I didn't know everybody already knew this, but wanted to keep the *skeleton in the cupboard!* Thanks to you, I get the picture. But

Bañez (whom you don't much like) is practically unobtainable; Soto, and that Tolet whom I knew about only through his commentary on Aristotle,[4] are impossible to find in print; and the sand is running low in the hourglass.[5]

You made me very happy by remembering me to C. A. Pegis and Father G. Smith, from Marquette. Pegis, a one-hundred-percent Greek, born Orthodox, converted by his Jesuit teachers, especially the Rev. J. F. Mc Cormick, is a close friend of Father Smith, who was one of my first students at the Toronto Institute. I assigned him a paper to do on I forget what point from Saint Bonaventure; I was getting ready to give him his mark as a student; but as soon as he began, I put aside my pen and paper to listen, spellbound. When he was ready to write a thesis, I asked him to do one on Molina, so I could be clear in my own mind on that subject. He did an excellent job, which, despite our entreaties, his Superiors never permitted him to publish.[6]

You have revealed to me a side of the Rev. Father Carlo Boyer I wasn't acquainted with, and right at the moment when I had been making an effort, if not superhuman, at least super-Gilsonian, to like him. At the last Thomist Congress but one[7] (in any case the last one I attended, under the authority of Father Garrigou[8] and the permanent censorship of Father Boyer), our Carlo took Pegis aside to explain to him *all* the passages in *Humani Generis* which he assured him were directed against you. "How do you know that?" asked Pegis. "Someone in authority must have told you this: who was it?" The Reverend Father kept mum.[9] I'm telling you these things, because it seems to me that with books like yours we are beginning to come out into the open, where *unimaginable* propositions, like Father Boyer's, p. 62, note 1, can no longer be formulated.[10]

I certainly wouldn't dare write what I nevertheless think: that all of this, Boyer included, is a sequel, or simply a manifestation, of the superficial philosophizing endemic to the Church from the beginning but which has infested Scholasticism since the thirteenth century. For every Saint Thomas and others like him, who magnificently destroyed the obstacle, or even hoisted and boosted themselves over it, there have been hundreds of low-grade "rationalists" who foundered on it. Father Boyer asked me one day for an article for an issue of *Doctor communis* (no relation to the *Universal Doctor!*), and proposed, among other possible subjects, the following two: (1) *Philosophia fundamentalis necessaria ad salutem;* (2) *Doctrina S. Thomae Aquinatis in omnibus sequenda.* My answer to him, more or less, was that both propositions were contradictory. I tried to say it tactfully in an article, but I'm not sure he understood.[11]

This is what is frightening: orthodoxy in the hands of her destroyers. The tragedy of modernism was that the rotten theology promulgated by its opponents was in large part responsible for modernism's errors. Modernism was wrong, but its repression was undertaken by men who were also wrong, whose pseudo-theology made a modernist reaction inevitable.[12]

I see redemption only in a Thomist theology as you perceive it, in the company of Saint Augustine, Saint Bonaventure, and the great theologians of the Christian East: they are all welcome because despite unavoidable *philosophical* differences, they all try to draw an *intellectus* from the same Faith. I wish I could unreservedly include Duns Scotus (to please my friend Father Balić)[13] and I do include him, certainly! but with one reservation: he taught that the object of *our* theology, for us men, is not God, but the *ens infinitum*. . . . And he seems to me to make the sight of God into the object of a *potentiality subject to nature* with no mystery to it, instead of the way it is with Saint Thomas, for whom the whole of the divine mystery is already present in the very nature of the intellect. There are but three "intellectual" beings: God, Angel, and Man. This is why the creation of *Man-intellect-image* makes sense only within the framework of the master-plan of creation. Of course God could have created man without raising him to the beatific vision! The real mystery, for me, is not just the Elect; but that

95

the Elect may not be all there are. Why does Dante speak of

le gente dolorose
c'hanno perduto il ben dell' intelleto?

I'm afraid I don't share your sympathy for the ideas of Blondel and Teilhard de Chardin, and that hurts me. I am not speaking of them as men, nor as Christians. I wish I were as good a Christian as Blondel, and Father Teilhard de Chardin was a model priest (which is nothing to sneeze at);[14] I am talking about their philosophico-theological styles. Let's leave Father [Teilhard] aside; he's been in *Match* and for a long time *Planète* has given him a place of honor in its "Magiciens du Matin"[15] [celebrity feature]; he was neither a theologian nor a philosopher; but Blondel was a philosopher who made himself into a theologian.[16] When I was young, he led me to think that Scholasticism[17] was a venture of "monophorism acting extrinsically". I really believed it. But if the creation is not an instance of monophorism acting extrinsically, then what is it? *Fecisti nos ad te; Quid habes quod non accepisti? Ipse prior dilexit nos,* etc., etc. Because of him, I considered *fides ex auditu* to be something like error, almost an ungodliness worthy of condemnation.[18] But make no mistake about it, the early Blondel, the only one that counts,[19] is also the one they would like to

96

(anyway they tried to) make into a sort of *Doctor Communis* in the major seminaries. He has my full respect, but it took him a long time to find his niche in Christian theological tradition;[20] and he never managed that, even at the end, without needing something to oppose in order to assert his position, without feeling constrained to create an enemy, however imaginary that enemy might have been, whom before all else he had to destroy. Often, he took the refutation of these contrived errors as a sufficient affirmation of the truth. I've run up against this more than once, because *he knew in advance that I was wrong;* I could tell you one or two funny stories to illustrate this point. I never gave him the satisfaction of a reply; a personal attack on him would not be my way of straightening him out, ever, but when they want to elevate him to the title *Doctor scholarum,* you must understand that all the same I'd have to blow the whistle.[21] Outside of that, he's welcome too, with his Catholic philosophy[22] that isn't a Christian philosophy but which, however, spontaneously and single-handedly discovers the divine message as if the Word of God had never existed.[23] It's exactly the converse of the thought of Newman, whom I call the last of the Fathers of the Church.[24]

*Claudite jam rivos. . . .*[25]

Please accept, reverend and dear Father, my

most sincere and enthusiastic compliments, together with the highest regard of

Your friend,

É. GILSON

[1] However, Dom Cappuyns, who had wholeheartedly approved *Surnaturel* in 1947, was to show a certain impatience in his recognition of my two volumes in 1965. For this fine historian, as for many others, the question was closed, and there was no interest in reopening it: *Bulletin de théologie ancienne et médiévale* 924 (October 1947). Cf. L. 1, n. 9.

*Le Mystère du surnaturel* was written only to develop, without changing the basic purpose, and following approximately the same outline, a long article published under the same title at the beginning of 1949 in *Recherche de science religieuse* 36:89–121. This article, carefully revised in Rome, had been approved by the censors, and the Father-General, J. B. Janssens, had heartily congratulated me on it. It was not a recapitulation nor a clarification of the book *Surnaturel,* but an enlargement; my goal was not to correct the book, but by adding some new citations from traditional sources, to explain and to justify the doctrinal conclusions which as yet had merely been touched upon in a few quick pages (the first work was really presented only as a series of "historical studies"). This 1949 article seems at first to have just about gone unnoticed. Even the very copious and extremely detailed *Bibliographie analytique et critique de Maurice Blondel* by René Virgoulay and Claude Troisfontaines, vol. 2, *Études sur M. Blondel* (Louvain, 1976), 229, no. 677, said of the 1946 *Surnaturel:* "Father de Lubac's book was to be rewritten and developed in 1965 (*Le Mystère du surnaturel*)." From then on the erroneous impression became ingrained. It will be noticed again in 1981 in Cardinal Siri's long, pathetic diatribe against this book. It gave rise to several myths. People thought they saw in the 1965 book an effort to correct, or at least to defend, the 1946 volume, with a view to making it more conformed to a sentence in the encyclical *Humani Generis* of August 1950. But on the contrary this encyclical was itself demonstrably inspired by my 1949 article, because it avoided invoking the so-called theory of "pure nature" that a number of theologians wanted the encyclical to validate. (If there had been a first draft, which I am not aware there was, its text would have been closely checked by competent, independent theologians.) Several readers immediately picked up on this; like this author of a letter dated September 25, 1950, who wrote to me: "The sentence in the encyclical about the supernatural is found word for word in the article in *Recherches,* pointed out as evidently false, because 'if God had so willed it, he could have denied us being, and to this being that he did give us, he could have utterly refused the vocation to see him face to face. If this terminology is inadequate, it is not so by reason of the sovereign liberty it recognizes in God. The contrary proposition suggests a double error. . . . Nothing either from outside him or from within him, could force God to grant me being; furthermore, nothing could make him endow my being with a supernatural character'", p. 104. Cf. the text of the encyclical: "Others distort the true concept of the gratuity of the supernatural order when they claim that God could not create beings invested with intelligence without calling and ordaining them to the beatific vision." I had said that again and again, in the conclusion of this same article in 1949.

As I had already said in the 1946 book: "The relationship of man and God should never be thought of as basically ruled by any natural law or any necessity whatsoever, be it internal or external. Everything in the gift that God wishes to make of himself, and consequently in the desire in our nature that results from God's gift, is explained by Love. Love is not necessarily a good which by its own nature is spread abroad: this is a personal Love that freely raises the being to whom he wishes to give himself. Nothing limits the sovereign autonomy of God who gives himself." And as far as the historical point of view is concerned, I observed in an end note to this article: ". . . Dom Cappuyns agrees . . . with the interpretations of Saint Thomas' doctrine that we have set forth. We dare to hope that his long-recognized authority on the matter will remove most of the objections people have presented to us, better than our own efforts at explanation could do. If difficulties still persist, we think they will be of the kind that by the same token impose themselves on every mind concerned with traditional thought, questions that will never go away, if it is true that every solution creates new problems. The truth of the Faith never ceases to stimulate and to redirect the activity of the intellect" (*RSR*, 1949: 80–121). This article was cited by Father Xavier Tilliette in his review of the 1965 book.

The 1949 article had had several other attentive readers. On July 19, 1950, Father Jean Daniélou wrote to me from Innsbruck: "In Vienna I saw von Ivanka, who was coming back from Rome where he had given a lecture at the Oriental Institute. Your name came up in our discussion and Father Hausherr vigorously defended you. Ivanka himself fully concurs with you. He liked your article on *Le Mystère du surnaturel* very much, with its notion, essential in his opinion, that the intellect is of the order of mystery and can't be treated as a manifestation of 'nature', at least in the modern sense of the word."

[2] Here, evidently, the principle is the same for Gilson as for Ivanka, and in his opinion it would have worked the

same way in Saint Thomas' thought. It is the idea Gilson expressed by saying, in *Le Philosophe et la théologie* (1960), 60, that concerning man "Thomist nature is not Aristotelian nature". In *Les Tribulations de Sophie* (1967), 33, he was to cite Bañez (1528–1604) again in this connection: "*Et hoc est quod saepissime clamat divus Thomas, et Thomistae nolunt audire.*" In fact, for Cajetan and the legion of Scholastics of every school who are his disciples, "*naturale desiderium non se extendit ultra naturae facultatem*": *In Primam*, q. 2, a. 1, n. 10, etc. In addition, it is the one Father Tonquédec was to use to counter Blondel, in the name of Thomism, orthodoxy, and the evidence itself: "A natural desire is essentially proportionate to nature", in *Deux Études sur la "Pensée"*, 149.

[3] Gilson went one better than my critique of Cajetan; I perhaps had suggested that he might soften his epithet "*corruptorium Thomae*" just a little. But he had noticed that in his famous commentary Cajetan did not give in "to any objective historical curiosity at all" (no "historicist" scruples on his part!). What Cajetan comments upon is not always "what Saint Thomas says, and one sees in him a kind of distancing of himself from the fundamental ideas" of his author: "The distinctions that he so glibly initiates have nothing to do with promoting a better understanding of Saint Thomas' thought; their purpose is rather to substitute his own": "Cajetan et l'humanisme théologique", in *Archives d'histoire doctrinale et philosophique du Moyen Age* (1955–1956) 22:118, etc. Earlier D. Soto, O.P. (1495–1560), had remarked, when the commentary first came out: "*Haec glossa destruit textum, est tortuosa, . . .*" and a number of others had denounced the commentator's infidelity to the master. Sestili said, at the end of the nineteenth century: "*Hac in re videtur apertissime a S. Thoma discidere*"; a judgment confirmed by the whole group of historians of theology: Martin, O.P. (*Ephe. th. lovan.*, 1924); Vallaro, O.P. (*Angelicum*, 1934); A.-E. Motte, O.P. (*Bulletin thomiste*, 1933); A. Raineri (*Divus Thomas*, Plac., 1936–1937),

etc. Canon Balthazar wrote in 1928 in *Criterion* 4:473: "One asks oneself how Cajetan had the nerve to propose his exegesis, and why it was, in point of fact, taken seriously for such a long time." Monsignor Antonio Piolanti in 1957, in *Divinitas* 1: Cajetan "separates" the natural and supernatural orders the way he separates himself from Saint Thomas. S. Dockx, O.P., in *Archives de philosophie*, 1964; 79–80: Cajetan "modifies the argumentation" and even "the text of Saint Thomas", etc. Suarez himself had said a long time before: "*Cajetanus et moderniores theologi tertium consideraverunt statum, quem pure naturalem appellarunt.*" Hence Gilson's ironic quip: "I didn't know everybody already knew this. . . ." Yet an enthusiastic coalition nonetheless united fanatical Suarezians and intransigent Thomists, even as they continued to bicker among themselves, in the first part of our century, so that they could exalt this *natura pura* on whose definition they hadn't a prayer of agreeing, and so that they could push to have it imposed on a level with dogma. It is amusing to see how each of them betook himself to this task. Father Descoqs, whose anti-Thomism was hardly a secret, found it necessary to turn to Cajetan as "a metaphysician and a theologian of the first rank", who knew how to give a "reasonable" explanation capable of redeeming his master's reputation (*Le Mystère de notre élévation surnaturelle*, 128–133); Father Boyer, who, as Dean of Theology at the Gregorian, represented at the time what tried to pass for official Thomism, proclaimed that "a (human) nature is an essence which *rests* in the portion of good allotted to it", but, undoubtedly knowing very well that Saint Thomas had said the opposite ("*non quiescit*") and not daring to assert his authority too explicitly, said only that "it stands to reason" (*Gregorianum* 28 [1947]: 300–301); the academic L. Jugnet found another argument: one ought to interpret Saint Thomas as Cajetan and the modern Scholastics do, because "any compromise on this point" would amount to making Saint Thomas an "Augustinian" (*Pour connaître la pensée de saint Thomas* [1949], 23), etc.

It is instructive to compare Cajetan with his predecessor Denys le Chartreux (1402–1471). Denys already upheld the same thesis as Cajetan, but for the purpose of refuting Saint Thomas openly, rather than claiming to comment upon him.

[4] François Tolet, S.J., born at Córdoba in 1533, died in Rome in 1596. Author of an *In Summam Theologiae Sancti Thomae Aquinatis Enarratio*, the fruit of a long teaching career at the Roman College, he had reedited and reorganized the manuscript continuously until just before his death. Like both the Dominican Soto and a little later the Franciscan Macedo, etc., he thought that the authentic philosophy of Saint Thomas on the destiny of man, which was also essentially that of Saint Bonaventure and Duns Scotus, should be reaffirmed in opposition to the innovative theses of Cajetan, whose gloss "destruit textum". In *In Primam*, q. 1, a. 1, ad 2, he refutes Cajetan's idea that "*capacitas*" is "*non naturalis sed obedientialis*"; in *In Priman Secundae*, q. 1, a. 8, he says: "*Si homo perfecte cognosceret naturam suam, cognosceret finem suum esse visionem divinam.*" No less than Saint Thomas, he asserts that God's gift of the beatific vision is absolutely free: "*gratuita voluntate creaturam rationalem beatificat . . .*" (*In Tertiam Enarratio* 3, q. 23, a. 2). Father Paria undertook to publish Tolet's *Enarratio* in 1869, but the project was never completed. Therein lies a problem not yet solved. The generation of Jesuits who came after Tolet adopted Cajetan's and Suarez' theses. Tolet upheld the ancient tradition until the beginning of the seventeenth century.

[5] Renaissance historians in Italy having attributed to Thomist doctrine a certain influence on Pomponazzi's reservations about the immortality of the soul, Gilson responded in 1959 that Pomponazzi's position was derived not from Saint Thomas but from Cajetan. Anxious to confirm his thesis, he took another trip to Venice in September 1960.

(He had been there in 1958 to take part in the International Philosophical Congress, and he would go again in 1964 to lecture at the Cini Foundation.) His purpose, on the 1960 trip, was to examine the earliest editions of Pomponazzi's works (Shook, *Gilson,* 353–354). Without specifically agreeing with Pomponazzi, Cajetan had declared his doctrine in conformity with Aristotle's and had offered a *non placet* against the decree of the Lateran Council (1513) that required philosophy professors to defend the conclusions of the Christian Faith in their lessons (Mandonnet, *DTC,* 2:2).

Although Cajetan's doctrine is reminiscent of that of the Averroists, he himself is "in no way one of them", but he finally realized "that his method justified all the more the possibility of the immortality of the soul, yet perhaps not so much, if one refers to the disillusioned texts near the end". However, he "put into circulation a Thomism tailored to the Aristotelian contours Saint Thomas had so cleverly avoided". If, nowadays, Gilson continues, "one has the temerity to question whether Saint Thomas' doctrine was essentially the same as Aristotle's, certain individuals get nervous, and sometimes may even become angry. These are usually the same ones who see no basic difference between Cajetan's teaching and that of Saint Thomas Aquinas" (*Cajetan et l'humanisme théologique,* 128–136). Gilson, however, gentleman and scholar that he was, made it clear that (ibid., 114): "Neither Cajetan personally nor the importance of his work is at issue. It is really naïve to blame a man for having done something other than what one might have preferred. One may, however, sometimes express a word of regret. . . ."

[6] See Appendix III.

[7] The Congress in Rome of September 11–17, 1950, the third of the international congresses organized by the Academy of Saint Thomas Aquinas, held one month after the publication of the encyclical *Humani generis.* The principal movers and shakers were Fathers Garrigou-Lagrange and

Boyer; their morning lectures which opened the Congress, as someone who attended them noted, came across as "directives", which distressed the whole group considerably. "The first, given by Father Garrigou-Lagrange, went over like a lead balloon; we sat through Father's tediously quoting the encyclical seven times. His presentation was entitled, '*De demonstratione existentiae Dei*'." He developed this subject in a manner so terribly boring that the friendly tone in his voice gave scant relief. It is true that the night before, in the course of a heated argument, Gilson had warned Garrigou-Lagrange that he would immediately interrupt him from the floor, despite all the rules and regulations, were he to insist on making certain inflammatory remarks. . . . Monsignor Parente's talk, "*De numere rationis ad finem hominis inveniendum*" (on the "natural" end of man) was also extremely simplistic; Father de Broglie, who sat next to me, could not keep from reflecting: "He dodges the issues too much; it is hard to show that Saint Thomas spoke of a natural end after this life: this is the main objection of the delegation from the University of Louvain and it's a serious one." There follows an account of an incident that provoked an official protest on the part of the group from Louvain, who put out the word that if the infringements of Fathers Garrigou-Lagrange and Boyer were allowed to stand, they would walk out. A number of Dominican theologians mentioned their own differences with Garrigou-Lagrange in private caucuses. There is a description of another "lively dispute" in a letter from Father Stanislas Lyonnet, dated September 30, 1950.

Gilson's lecture (on the evidence of the "*De ente et essentia*") was the most brilliant at the Congress. . . . In conversation, Gilson protested the abuse of Scholasticism in the seminaries: "People are presenting Saint Thomas shorn of his religious character; they forget that he wrote at least once: '*Doctrina sancta non indiget philosophia*'; they pour the most abstract philosophy down the throats of student-priests too young to defend themselves—and young priests shouldn't have to; alienating the mystics, they interpret (or more often misinterpret) their philosophy any way that suits them. . . . For me, the guiding principle of my religion is not my Thomism, however sincere, but the prayer: '*Propitius esto mihi peccatori*'." He said all this before a group that grew in size as the moments passed. . . . (From the notes of a participant in the Congress.)

[8] On Father Garrigou-Lagrange (1877–1964): M.-B. Lavaud, "Le Père G.-L., in memoriam" (*Rev. thomiste* 64.2 [1964], 181–199); "Le Père G.-L. maître spirituel, témoignage d'un disciple et ami" (*Vie spirituelle*, Aug.-Sept. 1964: 337–354); J.-H. Nicolas, "*In memoriam, le Père G.-L.*" (*Freib. Zeitschrift* 11 [1964]: 390–395); E. Pérez: "*Personalidad filosofica-teológica del Reginaldo G.L.*" (*Teología espiritual* 8 [September 1964]: 447–462); *Angelicum* 42 (1965): 1–2: "*Reginaldi G.-L., in memoriam*" (the entire issue); H.-D. Gardeil, in *Catholicisme*, vol. 4: col. 1764, made mention of "the wide diversity of his writings, his brilliant teaching ability, his active participation in various Congregations in Rome", and Father Lavaud recalled "his outstanding pedagogical talent".

Among his numerous books: *Le Sens commun, la philosophie de l'être et les formules dogmatiques* (1918); *Dieu, son existence, sa nature* (1915); *De Revelatione ab Ecclesia proposita* (1918); *Perfection chrétienne et contemplation* (1929); *Les Trois Ages de la vie intérieure* (1938); *La Synthèse thomiste* (1946); *L'Amour de Dieu et la croix de Jésus* (1929). As a young Dominican, he had read the *Disputationes* of John of Saint Thomas aloud to his director, Father Dehau, who was almost blind: "As he read it aloud, it became for him the beginning of a long intellectual intimacy with the great commentator" (B. Lavaud). Even though he considered himself a loyal disciple of Saint Thomas, he was destined always to view him through the eyes of "Cajetan, Bañez, John of Saint Thomas, Billuart"; later on, he would become a fervent apostle of the notorious "twenty-four theses". In 1904, he took some courses at the

Sorbonne; on May 6, in Séailles' class, he was irritated by a presentation given by another student, "a Bergsonian, a great young lout with a very kind face, who looked like a Slav, with bushy hair, etc." (this turned out to be Jacques Maritain); he calmed down as he came to this conclusion: "All things considered, I hardly see anybody but young people taking an interest in the Bergsonian paradoxes." He had naïvely written to his mentor Father Ambroise Gardeil: "Have you read Blondel's article 'Histoire et dogme' in the *Quinzaine*? . . . People of that persuasion make up a considerable faction among the young clergy; and they hate us just as much as we hate them." (Youthful letters to Father A. Gardeil, published by F. von Funten, O.P., in *Angelicum* 42 [1965]: 166.) (Eighty years later, Father François Dreyfus, O.P., was to cite *Histoire et dogme* as a text he considered definitive for clarifying early Christian history and justifying the Faith of the Church, in his book *Jésus savait-il qu'il était Dieu?* [Cerf, 1984].) Thus, this young religious of twenty-seven, who could be pardoned, at that age, for his poor grasp of a confused state of affairs, this victim of erroneous judgment and a fiery temper, was innocently to instigate a bitter conflict that terrorized Blondel off and on right up to the approach of his death in 1949. Didn't Garrigou-Lagrange go so far as to threaten Blondel, regardless of his great age, with God's punishment in the next life, if he did not pronounce the public recantation Garrigou-Lagrange would dictate to him? (See Blondel, October 24, 1946; March 14, 1947; March 29, 1948, in Blondel and Valensin, *Correspondance* 3:227.)

After a brief teaching assignment at Saulchoir, Father Garrigou-Lagrange was called to Rome in 1909, to the Angelicum, which was being founded that year. Beginning in 1917, he gave a course in spirituality that he taught until 1959, and starting in 1919 he actively collaborated on the *Vie spirituelle* established by Father Vincent Bernadot. In the twenties and

thirties, he conducted a retreat every summer in the Dominican Sisters of the Presentation's chapel in Meudon. M. and
Mme. Jacques Maritain recruited the participants for these
retreats. His many polemics were just so many accusations.
Father Auguste Valensin, S.J., had written as early as 1913:
"From men who understand things the way Father Garrigou-
Lagrange does, one may expect just about anything, and the
minute one dares to give evidence of their lack of comprehen-
sion, one can be sure that they will take any explanation one
might give them as a personal insult." In 1935, he published
in *Angelicum*, an article on "the twenty-four Thomistic theses" on the occasion of "the thirtieth anniversary of their
approval", one more step, among others, in his scheme to
impose his intellectual dictatorship. The misery of the years
1940–1945 did not put a stop to his private war: in the course
of a lecture tour in France in 1942, he "sowed terror
everywhere he went". His new offensive, between 1946 and
1951, aroused bitter indignation, but the angry reactions only
fed the flames. He kept it up in the name of Thomism, which
was for him the only true faith. As his colleague Father Motte
observed (*Bulletin thomiste* 4:574), for him, it was "no use
reading the texts: Saint Thomas *cannot* have claimed. . . ."
Nevertheless, he read other texts wrong, believing he found
therein more heresies to be stamped out. The credibility he
enjoyed in spite of everything leaves one speechless, at a time
when, according to astute observers, he had fallen into dis-
credit. His only excuse is his own recklessness. The great
Stanislas Fumet, who possessed a fine sense of fair play and
remained a disinterested observer of these theological donny-
brooks, could not help writing in his memoirs (*Histoire de
Dieu dans ma vie* [1978], 639): There was "in this theologian's
makeup an amusingly childish touch". (More than once I
found myself saying to my friends: "I agree with Father
Garrigou more often than he agrees with me.")

Father Jean Daniélou wrote to me on April 6, 1949, when

he returned from Rome: "I've finally met Father Garrigou-Lagrange. It was utterly hilarious and I must confess those were the funniest moments of my stay in Rome. I can't decide whether he's more like a typhoon or a volcano erupting. . . . He spoke of you, about *Surnaturel*. Moreover, he sees little difference between you, Father Boyer, Father de Blic, or Father de Broglie. As far as he's concerned, none of you is worth two cents. . . . He remarked, however, . . . that we have to admit that your book wasn't quite clear. I asked him, under these circumstances, to give those who are searching the benefit of the doubt. He replied that in his youth he too had had problems, but that now everything was completely clear!" (Cf. Fumet, *Histoire,* 330: "Le Père Garrigou, homme sans inquiétude . . . ".)

[9] Father Shook has preserved various incidents that took place at this Congress in more detail. Before it officially opened, Father Garrigou, accosting Gilson in the middle of a little knot of people, told him he was getting ready to take a shot at him on account of his recent book on *L'Être et l'Essence,* for claiming that metaphysical truths can change: a very dangerous assertion. . . . Suspecting a threat of being put on the Index, Gilson replied: "If you do that, I'll walk out of the Congress and be back in Paris the same day." A similar incident on the following day, in front of all the members in the plenary session: Father Boyer, who was chairman, announced that the report Van Steenberghen had just read deserved to be censured, and called on the next speaker. Whereupon the Dean of Louvain, De Rayemaeker, stood up and demanded to know on whose authority he was establishing himself as censor: Boyer had to apologize. According to Shook, a "deeper" gloom took hold, when it was learned that outside of the meeting but speaking in his capacity as chairman, Boyer had stated that as a result of the encyclical *Humani generis,* the Holy Office was going to put the book *Surnaturel* on the Index. Shook has reproduced the account

that Pegis gave him: "Boyer showed me in a copy of *l'Osservatore Romano* the text of *Humani generis* in which a paragraph was underlined, and asked me if I knew against whom this paragraph had been written. I said I had no idea, and then he avowed that it was against de Lubac. I'm sorry I did not reply by insisting on knowing how he got that information. But in the event, I was prepared for what Gilson told me that night . . .: they were making noises about trying to get *Surnaturel* put on the Index" (June 24, 1975). (It was to place these details in a larger context, Shook continues, that Gilson wrote to Father de Lubac several years later . . . [pp. 299–301].)

I later discovered there was more to it than that. Having been filled in by his personal advisor, Father (later Cardinal) Augustin Bea, S.J., on what was going on, Pius XII immediately sent me by Father Bea written confirmation of his complete confidence and encouragement. In the end, the experience taught me that even the finest people are capable of going to extremes when caught in a supercharged atmosphere. The confused memory of the modernist crisis made a number of theologians mistrustful; it caused them to suspect as more or less hypocritical the language used by the young men who upset them most. Later, I witnessed a restoration of cordiality and peace between one and another of them.

[10]Carlo Boyer, S.J., *Cursus philosophiae,* vol. 2, *Ethica generalis,* q. 1, "De fine moralitatis", art. 5, "Utrum Deus sit beatitudo hominis": "*Doctores christiani omnes ut veritatem philosophicam habent, quod beatitudo hominis solum in possessione Dei inveniatur . . .*" (p. 454). Cited in *Le Mystère du surnaturel,* 62, n. 1: "The great traditional texts on man's destiny and blessedness were to be systematically refuted in favor of a natural plan that distorts them. They were to be understood from this point on as nothing but affirmations of purely natural philosophy. The 'perfection' of human nature to which these very texts apply . . . was itself going to be, in

the same way, a fully natural perfection; pure philosophy was supposed to furnish the concept of natural perfection, etc." Other texts in *Surnaturel* (1946), 438–447: "Vision naturelle immédiate".

[11] "Sur deux thèmes de reflexion" (1960). (Cf. *Documentation catholique* 10 [1957]: 155–164: Boyer.) On the complications that ensued because of the mixups Boyer created, see Shook, *Gilson,* 330–331, 354–355: ". . . Father Boyer brought on an insoluble problem when he (and not *Humani generis*) asserted that there was one basic philosophy necessary for salvation. What Father Boyer did not know is that any philosophy that partakes of theology, is theology" (Pegis to Van Ackeren).

[12] Gilson will again write about the 1950 Congress and its atmosphere, in 1967 in *Les Tribulations de Sophie*: "When I went to Russia in 1919, the local Saint Thomas there was called Karl Marx. . . . Sometimes it scares me to think that some people describe the status of Thomism in the Church as being like that of Marxism in Communist countries. If that were the case, it would really be terrible and, for me, intolerable; but is it really that bad? . . . Saint Thomas is essentially and before all else a theologian . . ." (pp. 17–54).

[13] Father Charles Balić, O.F.M., Yugoslavian (Croatian), professor and rector in Rome (Antonianum), one of the main representatives of the Scotist School, *peritus* at Vatican II. In the course of the work of the theological commission preparatory to the Council (1960–1962), he was the principal compiler of the chapter on the Virgin Mary intended at first to conclude the already prepared Constitution on the Church. The sub-committee he more or less chaired (and to which he had invited me) having produced a text that was much longer than they had originally envisioned, the commission decided in the end that the chapter should be presented as an independent document. The Council was to put it back into the arrangement the preparatory commission had worked

with at the outset: *Lumen gentium,* chap. 8 and last, *"De beata Maria Virgine Deipara . . . in mysterio Christi et Ecclesiae".* See Appendix V.

[14] Gilson was always consistent in his high personal regard for various men with whom he did not agree (on Blondel, as late as 1967, in *Les Tribulations de Sophie,* 64: "The man himself was too great to eulogize"). That way, he could feel more at ease within the carefully circumscribed area where he did not allow himself to make judgments: namely, the area of "philosophico-theological *style".*

[15] Gilson paid too much attention to the raucous and absurd popularizations in magazines like *Match, Planète,* etc., that projected, in those days, a totally false picture of Teilhard's thought. This spurious "Teilhardism" was (and still is, at times) advocated by enthusiasts as fanatical as they are incompetent. Since it spread especially rapidly after his death (at Easter 1955), Father Teilhard could neither delineate what he really believed nor even give the needed explanations. Quite a few doctrines were attributed to him that were the reverse of his own thought as he had expressed it many times. See several important examples in H. de Lubac, preface by Michel Sales, *Teilhard posthume. Réflexions et souvenirs, . . .* (Fayard, 1977). Cf. L. 16, n. 7.

[16] Gilson had begun his university teaching career under the aegis of Lévy-Bruhl, as a historian of philosophy. Twenty-five years earlier, Blondel had clashed, from the moment he passed the oral examination, with a hostile philosophy; and he had stood up to it bravely, answering the "principle of immanence" that Léon Brunschvicg had made "the basis and precondition of every philosophical doctrine". In developing his own philosophical system Blondel very soon was to touch on theological problems, which obliged him to fight, so to speak, "on two fronts". He hoped for nothing better than to remain a philosopher and "not to meddle with religious questions except as far as they concern

philosophy, even if it meant being drawn, because of that, into a spot he never would have chosen deliberately" (Virgoulay, *Blondel et modernisme*, 184). He was to write, near the end of his life: "I never pretended to be a theologian and I am still just a simple believer, faithful to the Church as she herself is taught" (October 23, 1945).

[17] Gilson is forgetting (or wants to forget) that the "Scholasticism" so criticized (especially in 1910–1912 in the articles by *Testis* in *La Semaine sociale de Bordeaux*) was a Scholasticism typical of the twentieth century, the same kind he too had often been rather hard on, as his own letters bear witness (even this one: "orthodoxy in the hands of her destroyers"!). Cf. Blondel to Wehrlé, October 21, 1917: "The more I've studied Saint Thomas, the more I've noticed the exquisite torture our neo-Thomists force him to undergo . . ." (Blondel and Wehrlé, *Correspondance* 2:531). Étienne Borne was correct when he wrote: "Blondel knew how to use his Augustinian critical abilities to wither the corrupt, hybrid Thomism produced by grafting integrism onto Maurrassianism; and genuine Thomism learned to profit from the excellent results Blondel achieved" (*La Pensée politique de M. Blondel*, Centre d'archives M. Blondel, journées d'études, November 9–10, 1974 [Louvain, 1977], 61). Without claiming to involve himself in historical research, didn't Blondel anticipate Gilson's analyses when he wrote in 1913: "If . . . I were to take a historian's stance, wouldn't I be in a better position to point out . . . how easy it is to make a mistake in crediting Saint Thomas with the idea of defining, of 'codifying' 'pure nature' as opposed to 'supernature'?" ("Bernard de Sailly", *Comment réaliser l'apologétique intégrale?* [1913], 180.) And did he not sound even more like Gilson when he said how sorry he was that in "so many works that boast of being *ad mentem Divi Thomae*, what they actually give us is bad Thomas Reid, reeking of false Cartesianism, ersatz Biranism, dubious Cousinism?", a "poor man's rationalism"; and when he

registered his distress at seeing how many people wanted to raise this pseudo-Thomism to the power of "an administrative process where they would run philosophy like an intellectual junta"? (*Testis* [1910], 41, 49.) It also seems as if Gilson, in calling to mind the passing illusion of his youth, is letting himself fall under the spell of times gone by, when he moved in Laberthonnière's circle, where there was a hostility to Saint Thomas that Blondel never espoused.

One can say the same thing about Blondel and Gilson as Mlle. Marie-Thérèse d'Alverny said about Gilson and Massignon: "It was their own genius that kept them apart" (*Cahiers de civilisation médiévale*, vol. 22 [1979], 4, fasc. 8).

[18] Each of these two judgments seems to me to rest on a mistake in interpretation. The act of creation clearly cannot be compared here with the act of revelation, which requires the existence of a creature to whom the Creator may make the revelation; and Blondel never cast doubts on the necessity of *fides ex auditu*. A similar misunderstanding mars this sentence in *Les Tribulations de Sophie*, 61: ". . . as if there had never been any Christian teaching that defined revelation, grace, or, to come to the point, God's gift of himself as like the rush of a wave onto the shore; but in a unique sense: as a gift given *without any return to the giver*" (my italics). It wasn't a question of that; whatever one thinks of the solution, the problem Blondel confronted was something else altogether.

[19] This determination, however blunt it may seem, should be kept in mind when evaluating the discussions that have arisen among Blondel scholars on the relative merits of the early versus the later Blondel. See, among others, Henri Bouillard, S.J., "L'intention fondamentale de Maurice Blondel et la théologie", *Recherches de science religieuse* (1949), 321–402; *Blondel et le christianisme* (Seuil, 1961); "Le dernier chapitre de l' 'Action', 1893, éd. critique", *Archives de philosophie* 24 (1961): 29–113; "Philosophie de l'action et

logique de la foi", ibid., 27 (1964); *Ce que la théologie doit à la pensée de Maurice Blondel,* Centre d'archives M. Blondel, journées d'inauguration, March 30–31, 1973, pp. 41–48, etc. See also Virgoulay, *Blondel et modernisme.* A posthumous volume of the writings of Father Henri Bouillard is in preparation.

[20] The young Blondel really had an easier time finding a niche in the "spiritual" Christian tradition than in the properly so-called "theological" tradition. The teachers who were responsible for the profound significance of Blondel's inspiration were men like Saint Paul, Saint Augustine, Saint Bernard, Saint Ignatius Loyola. However, he had begun rather early in his carteer to read Saint Thomas, whom Father Beaudoin (*socius* of the Master-General of the Dominicans) had recommended to him; and Father Beaudoin was Blondel's trusted friend and confidant. In 1895, Blondel had spent a short while visiting the Roman universities. Numerous notes of his on Saint Thomas have been preserved (the earliest ones date from April 1899); these notes came from his reading of the works printed in the Leonine edition. In connection with his own work in philosophy he developed a considerable attachment to the *Contra Gentiles*: "If my critics would just meditate a bit on two texts from Saint Thomas, *CG* I, 2, 4 and the beginning of the brief work X, perhaps they would take a slightly less severe view of my attempts" (to Father Valensin, March 2, 1904). And "isn't it Saint Thomas who, exalting the method of the early Church Fathers, the 'major mode' of Apologetics, . . . praised the good and effective use of perseverance in winnowing from the chaff the grain of truth that will dispel insincerity and doubt and promote salutary acts of faith; *Ex dictis singulorum errantium rationes assumere ad eorum errores destruendos: CG* I, 2" (May 1904), etc. In 1908–1909, he told Valensin how he kept up his daily program of systematically reading Saint Augustine and Saint Thomas. In 1911–1912, he gave a departmental course on

the *Contra Gentiles*, and taught it again in 1916–1917. In 1912 he persuaded the ministry of Public Instruction to place some of Saint Thomas' texts on the required reading list for the Licentiate. In 1913–1914, he gave a series of public lectures "glorifying Saint Thomas and portraying Descartes at his feet, the way Averroës had once been depicted as a footstool" (at Brémond, December 27, 1913). About 1912, he applied himself to showing that Saint Thomas, "consistent with tradition, discerned two kinds of knowledge, corresponding to two functions of thought: there is an abstract and 'notional' knowledge, and a 'real' knowledge; *cognitio per connaturalitatem, per habitum, per unionem*". By 1923, he was teaching a course on "What we owe to Saint Thomas" and lecturing on Saint Thomas to the Provincial Union of Catholics in Public Education. In 1910, he contrasted two "Thomisms": "The first is an instrument of truth, of research, of ethical conduct; the second, one that many wish to turn into an administrative process that will set them up as an intellectual junta" (*Monophorisme*, 49); "I discovered when I contradicted some neo-Thomists, I was, without knowing it, working for the original, profound meaning of Saint Thomas." On March 14, 1914, he confessed to Wehrlé his "increasing horror of Cartesianism" and his desire to contribute to the revival of Thomism, etc.

Gilson is right to assert that Blondel was not a historian of theology or medieval philosophy. It does not follow that he was not, from his youth up, within Catholic tradition, nor that Catholic tradition did not significantly affect his philosophy. In a surprising vignette in his autobiography, looking backward from his own time to that of his teachers and his teachers' teachers, Gilson tells us that in those days, among young Catholics, "there was absolute ignorance of sacred studies", that a "brand-new Ph.D. in philosophy, if he knew his catechism, considered himself authorized to settle any theological dispute whatsoever"; "one of the salient traits" of "Catholic philosophy in the universities" of that era was "that, among so many Catholic philosophers—including Lachelier, Delbos, Maurice Blondel and others—not even one had ever studied theology, although they never felt the smallest qualm about involving themselves in theological matters. . . . These young laymen . . . didn't even think there was anything to be gained from studying theology" (*Philosophe et la théologie*, 72–73). Now here we have an odd grouping. Blondel is lumped together, on the one hand, with a younger philosopher and mathematician, Le Roy, whose ideas he ceaselessly opposed (cf. Blondel to Valensin, June 23, 1930), and, on the other hand, with an older man whose attitude was categorically counter to Blondel's, namely, Jules Lachelier. Lachelier's philosophy contains not a word about theology, nor indeed about the Catholic Faith, in spite of his being a very sincere, practicing Catholic himself; only the tiniest glimmer, for example on the last page of his *Fondement de l'induction* (*Oeuvres*, vol. 1 ([Alcan, 1933], 92) perhaps might suggest that a second philosophy, a "spiritual realism, open to an act of moral trust" could take the place of "materialistic idealism". . . . Blondel's intention was precisely to react against this academic hesitancy to approach theological questions. His plan was to impose on the philosopher, by means of an internal dialectic, consideration of the religious problem—without, however, giving the philosopher *carte blanche* to theologize any way he pleased! As for Delbos, Blondel's friend, this historian of philosophy's academic reserve was so pronounced that he would have been the last man on earth to attempt to play at being a theologian. Neither Lachelier's compartmentalized dualism that resembled in some ways the Parisian Averroists' "double truth" of olden times, nor, on the other extreme, the tactless heartiness of a few "Ph.D.s" who had the gall to call themselves theologians, was comparable to "Blondelism" at any stage in its development.

[21] A proper concern that turned out to be still more justified with regard to Teilhard. Moreover, neither one of them ever took it into his head to play the role of unique *doctor scholarum*. Infatuations, always more or less out of proportion, on the part of the young clergy (and sometimes their teachers too), are nothing unusual. Wasn't this true in Bergson's case? In addition, infatuations aside, one may conclude that Blondel's influence in the seminaries and among young priests was often all to the good. "From one end of his career to the other, he showed the greatest respect for faithfulness to Christian tradition. This fidelity was so real and so noticeable that, at a time of crisis, when the Church authorities were especially vigilant, when sincere Christians frequently fell into error on important matters of Faith, Blondel, although certain theologians made it their business to attack him with violent criticisms and even denunciations, was never officially censured in any way; on the contrary, he had the support of the highest ecclesiastical powers. His opinions . . . threw light on the Church's most pressing problems in his day: the correlation of faith and reason, of history and dogma, of social structure and missionary needs. His work played a primary role. Undoubtedly, more than anyone else, he helped many people get through the modernist crisis. We are still reaping the benefits of his influence upon theology. Now that early and perhaps inevitable misunderstandings have been cleared up, it is no longer a time to hang back; it's time we showed Blondel a little appreciation" (Henri Bouillard, S.J., *Recherches de science religieuse* [1949], 402).

[22] At the time, Blondel preferred the idea of "Catholic philosophy" to that of "Christian philosophy". For that reason, he entitled his 1932 work that recast some of his previous writings: *Le Problème de la philosophie catholique*, Cahiers de la Nouvelle Journée, 20. He admitted, however, that "the epithet *Catholic* attached to the word *philosophy* is still ambiguous in some ways and needs to be used with

great care and discretion, *secundum quid* and not *simpliciter*"; in his conclusion, he confessed to "an increasing sensitivity to the complexity of the problem". See, in the Blondel *Bibliography* by R. Virgoulay and C. Troisfontaines, vol. 1 (Louvain, 1975), 122–130, the different names Blondel was weighing and considering, according to the changes in his point of view, for his philosophy, between 1896 and 1934 ("integral philosophy"). In a long article in the *Revue de métaphysique et de morale* (1930), 423–469, that Xavier Léon had asked him to write for the fifteenth centenary of Saint Augustine's death, he mentions Gilson's "perceptive *Introduction à l'étude de saint Augustin*", published in 1929. In the same publication, in 1931, pp. 599–606, he responds to Émile Bréhiers article, "Y a-t-il une philosophie chrétienne?", ibid., 133–162.

²³ Here Gilson alludes to one of Blondel's letters, addressed to the Société française de philosophie (*Bulletin* [1951], 88): ". . . Should philosophical doctrines . . . be viewed as sufficient unto themselves, *buttoned down* . . . ? Or rather . . . should philosophy come to realize . . . how it creates a void within and beyond itself that makes room not merely for subsequent discoveries . . . , but for clarifications and contributions whose real source it is not, nor can it become? Now, it is this second thesis . . . that, although it does not proceed from revelation, is the only one in utter, unconstrained accord with Christianity." Gilson's interpretation does not fit; cf. n. 18, above. The suggestion of a Christian body of dogma arrived at immediately by reflective analysis of the subject was nowhere near what was in Blondel's mind. See, further, *Le Problème de la philosophie catholique*, 132, note. Gilson's article, "Le Problème de la philosophie chrétienne", published in 1931 by *La Vie intellectuelle*, became in 1932 the first chapter of *L'Esprit de la philosophie médiévale;* see also ibid., 21 (1933): "Autour de la philosophie chrétienne, la spécificité de l'ordre philosophique." The Dominicans in Juvisy organized on this theme, in September 1933, the second series of their "Thomist

Society Study Days". See, further, *Le Problème de la philosophie catholique*, 132, note. Blondel complained privately to Father Auguste Valensin, in a latter dated March 17, 1931: "How I need your advice on the precise and exact concept of Christian philosophy! I want to respond to it, but I'm always brought up short, and forced to give my answer willy-nilly and double-quick. Gilson, taking aim at 'the Augustinians', either ignores me or makes me look like a fool, paying no mind to page 468 in the *Revue de métaphysique* of last December. Besides, I wasn't being an Augustinian there at all, where my thoughts were picking their way toward refuge in the shelter of this great name, because my ideas didn't really come from Saint Augustine, they were trying to come to me from Christ. But Gilson has no time for *a* Christian philosophy or *the* Christian philosophy; he sees systems that are more or less Christianized, or placed side by side in history with Christianity, as closed concepts, each fixed precariously in its proper place in the historical order. Oh, historicism! It makes me groan to have to give it an answer, because every time I stick my neck out, I get my head chopped off." Again on August 21: "I've spent these last few weeks working on the problem of Catholic philosophy in response to Gilson's and Bréhier's offensives." At last, on October 10: "I knocked myself out on *Cahier 20*, which I had promised to Nouvelle Journée; and two weeks ago the manuscript was turned over to Archambault-Gay with this title: 'Le Problème de la philosophie catholique'. On top of that I had to correct the proofs of my letters to Gilson and Bréhier on the same subject, the first for the *Bulletin de la Société de philosophie* (relating to their March 21 meeting), the other for the *Revue de métaphysique;* this latter one won't come out until the Oct.-Dec. issue; Léon wants to put out the number dedicated to the hundredth anniversary of Hegel first."

[24] Blondel acquired his partial and somewhat sketchy knowledge of Newman rather late. His work was done in

an atmosphere completely unlike Newman's, so any comparison betweeen the two men's philosophies would be pretty pointless; but one can recognize a spiritual kinship in the two of them. Blondel very much admired Newman, and in this Gilson joined him. Gilson wrote an introduction for an edition of the *Grammar of Assent* (New York, 1955), 7–21. On Newman and Blondel: Henri Bremond, "Autour de Newman", *Annales de philosophie chrétienne* 155 (January 1908): 359–365.

[25] This lengthy, explosive passage is explainable, at least in part, by the remembrance of an already outdated spat (1931–1932) over the idea of Christian philosophy, brought on by repercussions from an article by Émile Bréhier (*Revue de métaphysique et de morale*, 1931). Gilson had aired his own views in a report to the Philosophical Society (March 21). Blondel, who had published his critique of Bréhier in the *RMM* (1931), 133–162, had fired off his objections to Gilson's report in the letter mentioned above (*Bulletin de la société française de philosophie*, 1931), and had answered Gilson's nettled response to this letter with yet another letter. Gilson thought he saw in the publication of Blondel's two letters with the Hegel issue in between, a ploy on Blondel's part to have the last word, but in fact this deed in the *RMM* was done by Xavier Léon, the secretary, who sincerely liked both men. See the detailed account of this business in Shook, *Gilson*, 198–201. In *Le Problème de la philosophie catholique*, 129, Blondel had written a little later on: "M. Gilson will forgive me for adding my clarification to his essay, for he has the double merit of historical erudition and philosophical rigor", but this left-handed compliment was Blondel's prelude to calling his "attempt at doctrinal historicism" insufficient. In his appreciation of this work in *Les Nouvelles littéraires* (May 7, 1932), Henri Gouhier said he was afraid that "by barring the way M. Étienne Gilson has opened, M. Blondel may be cutting off an effort that could become the

natural introduction to his own—and indeed, an undertaking without which his may turn out to be impossible"; a remark made advisedly, as an attempt at reconciling both men.

Monsignor Daniel Pézeril, who was then a student, was present at the meeting of the Philosophical Society. "Brunschvicg, who was at the time a kind of crown-prince of philosophy at the Sorbonne, was there", he tells us, "together with Bréhier, my 'patron' [Father Laberthonnière] who still looked tense; Édouard Le Roy, Maritain, and, at the back of the room, surrounded by young people, standing because he was short of stature, his cane in his hand, looking pugnacious and making comments under his breath, Gabriel Marcel. . . ." Everybody was biting his tongue to keep from mentioning Father Laberthonnière's name as the debate raged on. Yet, wasn't it his "Augustinian concept" that "Gilson the Burgundian cheerfully, carelessly, and cruelly made fun of . . .?" That, at least, was the impression Laberthonnière took away with him, and confided to his young visitor a few days later, reiterating his position "forcefully": "Christianity is my whole philosophy, just as it was for Justin Martyr. The originality of the gospel is that it reveals a moral bond between God and man. . . . The idea of an independent Christian philosophy came from the Middle Ages. . . ." Obviously, he and Gilson did not construe the word "philosophy" in the same sense; he surely must have been the one Gilson had in mind when he dreamed up the reproach of having "identified natural and supernatural as concrete terms, and worse, having refused to break the concrete down into concepts", that is to say, having been willing to "give them the only possible philosophical translation" (*Revue de l'Institut catholique de Paris*, Oct.-Dec. 1983: 238–240). Father Laberthonnière, as the interested party, could not have been mistaken about what Gilson said, and the sharp reply he repeated to young Pézeril was not merely defensive: it was a radical denial of Gilson's position, boiling up from the depths of his mortally wounded soul. This verbal breach between the two of them had been impossible to mend for a long time now, because at the bottom of it lay a basic and mutual disagreement.

Laberthonnière kept himself to himself. But Blondel, who was more of a philosopher, insisted on his point, and Maritain, who had participated in the debate at the Society, published a short treatise in 1933: *De la philosophie chrétienne.* This made it a three-dog fight, which I tried to break up with a 1936 article. Avoiding any attempt to smooth things over, I wanted to show that the three positions need not be mutually exclusive just because they were different or sounded confrontational, since they were three solutions to three distinct problems, with each problem occasioned by a separate set of circumstances. For Maritain, faithful to his own brand of Thomism and devoted to keeping his orderly distinctions each in its proper pigeonhole, the main thing was to admit that the Christian, when philosophizing, could get efficacious stimulation and comfort from his Faith to guide his rational thought-processes, as if his thought were being engineered from somewhere outside himself. To Gilson, who paid more attention to history, Christian revelation had been confirmed throughout the centuries as the mother of reason, and that proved that there could be a real philosophy that found its origin in Christianity; but wouldn't this philosophy stop being specifically Christian as soon as it became an activity of reason alone, at the moment when it could be called purely "philosophy", in the current sense of the word? It was this point that didn't seem to me to have been sufficiently cleared up. Finally, for Blondel—who, as we have seen, had no use for the expression "Christian philosophy"—but who cared little enough for straining his eyes to see the far-off Christian origins of a philosophy that was completely secular, walled up in the very profanity with which Blondel clashed, what had to be done was to undertake anew to convince philosophy that to be faithful to its purpose, free of irrational and confining bias, it should come out, by itself, step by step, by digging the "void" that Christian revelation would fill. However, at the same time, Blondel was starting on a new search, that, in a sense closer to the work of Gabriel Marcel than to Gilson's, was to bring him nearer to seeing the Faith as mother of philosophy. This was what made me write to him, on April 8, 1936, thanking him for sending me his new book, *L'Être et les êtres:* "It seems to me that I could have added, or rather, perhaps, completed, a paragraph (at the end of my article), by summarizing the last few pages at the end of your book. For . . . never more than with your latest work have we had Christian philosophy." See also *Exigences philosophiques du Christianisme*, posthumously published in 1950, part of it written as far back as 1930.

Having witnessed the path this new trend took as it developed in the "trilogy" by "the second Blondel", Étienne Borne was able to tell the French Philosophical Society on January 25, 1975: "Considered in relation to Christianity, philosophy is not reduced to the function of a preamble or preliminary. . . . Blondel as a Christian finds philosophy at the open end of a descending dialectical reasoning process. He begins with revelation and faith in the Word; then, after having offered solutions to a number of antinomic difficulties, the end product of his thought issues in philosophy." Borne illustrates Blondel's achievement in this manner: "Certainly, no one could extrapolate God the Holy Trinity from the philosophical idea of the absolute, for God the Holy Trinity is of a different order. But Plato had already dealt, in *The Sophist*, with this logical impasse, where one encounters the apparently contradictory necessity of attributing to the absolute both life and a Name. Applying Plato's work to the perspective of the Christian God, Blondel found a new way of putting the *Fides quaerens intellectum* into practice" (*Bulletin*, pp. 9–10).

(In 1983 the collectively-authored book *Pour une philosophie chrétienne*, Le Sycomore series [Paris-Namus: Lethielleux], the product of a colloquium held at Namur in a peaceful atmosphere, gave new life to the theme and opened new ways to look at it; the book contained a preface by P. P. Druet, "Problématique" by Simon Decloux, chapters by H. Urs von Balthazar, C. Bruaire, G. Chantraine, P. Henrici, K. Neufeld, X. Tilliette.)

In a communication presented at the Eighth International Thomist Congress (1981), the Rev. Paul Toinet wondered whether Gilson's opinions of Blondel had always been really "pertinent and fair". He stated his regret that the great "philosopher and historian" (whom he admired in both capacities) might not have known how to do full justice to the man who had bravely stood up to "the censure that secularized orthodoxy had taken charge of exercising", a man whose work stands, in our judgment, as a monument to the debate that cropped up over and over "between the *fides quaerens intellectum* and self-sufficient rationalism's addiction to its own power of academic excommunication". Moreover, he has us observe that perhaps Gilson may have contradicted himself somewhat by formulating most of his criticisms right after clearly explaining why it had been so difficult, not just for the preceding generation but for his own as well, to be in consonance with the great tradition of theology; anyway, it can't be made to stick that the author of *L'Action* intended to set aside any of the main, authentic theologies; nor that the sole result of Blondel's work was to create such confusion in so many bright minds. However, these reservations did not prevent the Rev. Toinet's being grateful that Gilson, without abandoning "his slightly brusque, good-humored manner, knew how to bulldoze his way through the complexity of the intellectual problems of his own day just as well as he could cut a path through the wilderness of ancient doctrines", so that what he said of his senior, "without taking everything into account, is by no means being negative" ("Philosophie catholique signe de contradiction", in *Studi Thomistici* 13, *Atti dell' VIII Congresso Tomistico internazionale*: 15–26, passim). Truthfully, Gilson did not neglect to give credit to "the admirable perspicacity Blondel exhibited in his critical analysis of Descartes' natural theology" (*God and Philosophy* [1941; 2nd ed. 1960], 88). Later, in contrast with the anti-Thomism displayed by a whole generation of clerics long forced to absorb Thomism in an adulterated form, he cited four laymen, among whom he named Blondel, and all four of whom were "products of secular education", who discovered on their own, each using his own method, each following his own route, the way back to the real Thomism (cf. a letter to Stefan Swiezawski, 1965; published in *Znak*, no. 303 [September 1979]: 939–940; reproduced in K. Rottenberg, *Sources franco-polonaises d'histoire religieuse*, vol 3 [Laski, 1982], 197). It is equally worth noting that Blondel and Gilson both grasped right away the true worth of Rousselot's thesis on *L'intellectualisme de saint Thomas d'Aquin* (1908), that cut across all the publications *ad mentem sancti Thomae* of the time. In closing, let me say only that this letter of June 21, 1965, so harsh and unfair to Blondel, is a letter of thanks totally approving a book which was called "Blondelian" by all and sundry. I said in it, on page 234: "By reason of the discussions it started, and even more the thoughtful conclusions a number of excellent minds reached because of it, Blondel's work contributed generously to bringing the theological tradition having to do with man's supernatural end to the forefront, and especially calling attention to the Thomist doctrine on matter."

Father L. K. Shook wrote to me from Toronto, on June 17, 1975, "I am becoming more and more convinced that one of Gilson's handicaps was not having appreciated Blondel."

## 10

6, rue Collet, Vermenton, Yonne

July 22, 1965

Reverend and dear Father and Friend,

Don't thank me! That wretched article, dominated by anxiety from not being able to do what was asked of me, had no value beyond that of a token of our friendship.[1] Besides, I'm about to give you another headache due to writing (it's already written . . . ) a critique of the work of your beloved Father Teilhard de Chardin. Coward that I am, I can't take responsibility for anybody else's *Teilhardinsis communis*. Lately, whenever I speak of the *Doctor communis*, obnoxious seminarians reproach me for not mentioning the great theologian[2] [Teilhard] in the same breath: the only great theologian, Father Congar says . . . (no, I'm wrong, he was talking about Blondel!)[3]— The worst thing is that I wrote the critique at the request of his Eminence, Cardinal Pizzardo. What it boils down to is that I've broken the vow I'd made to myself never to get involved with

Teilhard. . . . I think he's the most Christian of the gnostics.[4] At least, the critics will latch onto that word, and while they're busy with gnosticism they'll leave him in peace.

Further, I think I've figured out "meta-Christianity", but if it means what I now think it means, I wonder if your friend didn't just get a kick out of shocking people?[5]

"Consubstantial" is over and done with as far as I'm concerned,[6] but I got some very interesting letters out of it. . . .

Believe me, I remain

Very respectfully yours,

É. GILSON

---

[1] I had thanked him for his article published in *La Croix*. See Appendix II.

[2] Cf. L. 9, n. 21. Please note the date. It was before the last session of the Council; slogans had been bandied about in the press against "the pre-Conciliar Church" and in favor of a "renewed Church"; in Paris, as well as in Rome and elsewhere, pressure was being brought to bear to put in innovative and ambiguous texts; Saint Thomas had become the symbol of everything that had to go—and he hadn't always had the best of champions anyway: Gilson was the first to complain about that. Making use of a form of "Teilhardism" as a weapon against this unhealthy ferment, a "Teilhardism" as false as the "Thomism" that was being

rejected, were people against whom Teilhard, who had already been dead for ten years, had no way of protesting. One can understand how Gilson, finding the atmosphere created by "obnoxious seminarians" grating, and urged on by Cardinal Pizzardo, would have intervened. One can also see his conscientious effort (which, however, didn't do much good) to distinguish carefully between the "*Teilhardinsis communis*" and the real Teilhard—just as he insisted on the difference between the true "*Doctor communis*" and the grotesque caricature of Saint Thomas idolized by some and rejected by others. He wrote, in that same year 1965: ". . . Having taught their own versions of Thomism instead of Saint Thomas Aquinas himself, they now want to prohibit instruction in the real Thomism, in their headlong zeal to rid themselves of the false Thomism they had just finished forcibly installing in its place. . . ." "Among the anti-Thomists at the Council", he added, "you will find plenty of people who are against all philosophers, because somebody once tried to brainwash them with Saint Thomas' doctrine . . ." (to Stefan Swiezawski). Remarks made, of course, in private, in the heat of the moment, without much concern for moderation.

[3] Gilson's irritation is obvious, and the tenor of the times is explanation enough. No one but my friend Gilson would ever have supposed, even on the grounds of a misquoted or exaggerated slip of the tongue, that Blondel (or Teilhard) might have wooed Father Congar away from sound theology. See also Gilson's letter to Pegis, May 30, 1964 (in Shook, *Gilson*, 367).

[4] The tag was meant kindly, even as a compliment, but it doesn't make sense if "gnosis" is understood as it is currently today, as meaning the vast spiritual movement that from antiquity has corrupted the Christian Faith and that is still doing substantial harm even today, albeit in different form. Saint Irenaeus of Lyon, in his treatise *Contre les hérésies*, called it "pseudo-gnosis", or, as his editors Adelin Rousseau and

Louis Doutreleau translated it, "the gnosis whose very name is misleading" (*Sources chrétiennes*, 5 vol. [1969–1982]). It was a radically distorted form of Christianity. People began early to endeavor to find in Saint John's thought and vocabulary "a certain family resemblance to writings that smacked of gnosticism" (*Jerusalem Bible*, introduction to the writings of Saint John); they did the same thing with a few expressions used by Saint Paul (Ephesians and Colossians). Paul and John, on the contrary, are anti-gnostics in every particular; they exalt Jesus as the Word of God, by whom and for whom all things were made, "in whom all that came to be had life" (*JB*, Jn 1:4), "in his body lives the fullness of divinity" (*JB*, Col. 2:9). Accustomed as we are to these formulae, we hardly notice any more how shockingly daring they are, nor are we prompted to perceive in them the slightest whiff that might be redolent of suspect "gnosticism". In addition, John teaches us that "God is love" (*JB*, I Jn 4:8), and Paul, that "the love of Christ is beyond all knowledge" (*JB*, Eph 3:19). Teilhard, following in their train, has borne witness that the "unique" goal of all his work in this world was to make the world "see Jesus' face and love him"; in a project he was planning in 1937, he wanted to devote all his energies to "its final chapter on the Love of God" because everything else is merely "a pedestal made of rocks whose every feature we already know very well"; moreover, toward the end of his life, he intended to crown his work with a book all about the "Love of God".

Irenaeus understands perfectly that the fourth Gospel "is full of all kinds of bold statements"; but he observes that the "pseudo-gnostics' boldness" is not at all like Saint John's, for pseudo-gnosticism pops up everywhere "the way mushrooms shoot up from the ground": the pseudo-gnostics "weave artificial exegeses, trying to attract people with the glamor of their superior knowledge and incredible mysteries", they "confect a second Christ", descended from a

"Proto-Pater", and finally, as the end-product of "all sorts of complicated genealogies, they produce the 'Man', who utters the 'perfect secret knowledge'"; something one of them dares to call the "gospel of truth", that arrays itself against the Faith in God the Father, Jesus Christ the Son of God, and God the Holy Spirit, the Holy Trinity, one God (see the unabridged translation in one volume, by Dom Adelin Rousseau—not published as part of a collection—2nd ed. [Cerf, 1985]). This "gnosis" has, even in our century, some all-too-legitimate heirs—who have nothing in common with Teilhard. It would be arbitrary to insist that one must "speak not of his faith, but of his teachings" to appropriate to oneself the right to affirm that for Teilhard "gnosticism runs parallel to the Christian religion"; and if one wonders what will become of "the Christ of history in his new functions" assigned to him by Teilhard, one might just as well ask Saint Paul the same thing, taking out of context any verse at all from the Epistle to the Colossians that has to do with the cosmic role of Christ (cf. *Les Tribulations de Sophie*, 68, 157). Gilson was quite right to react (along with Maritain) against the tyranny of the "ideosophies" [philosophies of self] spawned by the Hegelian gnosis. Teilhard was no less allergic to this sort of thing, as much because of his realist instinct as because of his faith. And how amazing his depth of insight, born of long years of study and profound reflection, that led him to write to his Superior, on the threshold of the Second World War, having encountered so many politicians, economists, scientists, and all the other "gnostics" of our times, that beneath the readily evident causes of mankind's wars, the root of the evil can be traced to "the latent fact that people have given up believing in a personal God"! It is truly regrettable that Gilson never was able to spare a few hours from his own work to get to know him and become more familiar with his method and approach, that was in no way unwarranted: he would have found Teilhard to be neither historian nor metaphysician, but his accurate judgment would not have failed to perceive, among other things, that realism of his, his "yes" to being, his deep "love of being" in which he prayed God to keep him always, the love that bound him, as it did his friend Pierre Rousselot, to Saint Thomas Aquinas. But if we take note that Gilson saw the author of the *Proslogion* as a representative of "Christian gnosticism", a label he borrowed from Filliatre, who used it without pejorative intent ("Sens et nature de l'argument de saint Anselme", *Archives*, 1934: 51), we shall be able to say that once and for all, he has placed Teilhard in very good company.

[5]Cf. L. 9, n. 1. This new characterization does not fit Teilhard's personality at all. At least it shows that Gilson, who was a good man, promised not to take this really unfortunate word amiss.

[6]Not having really got through to those who had the ability or the authority to do something about it, Gilson soon became discouraged. But several of his latter works demonstrate that he was always sensitive to distortions and perversions of Christian thought, by no means rare occurrences in our country. On less crucial matters—small innovations or the taking of minor liturgical liberties—he exhibited merely annoyance or amusement, depending on how he felt that day. I heard a story he told one day, when he was in a very happy mood, with a mischievous gleam of mock-indignation in his eye, about a little girl, who, at Mass, had spotted him in his quiet and solitary corner, and at the moment of the passing of the "Peace", had run back to him and thrown her arms around his neck. There is a slightly different version— which does not contradict this one—in *Les Tribulations de Sophie*, 139–140.

## 11

6, rue Collet, Vermenton, Yonne

April 7, 1967

Reverend and dear Father and Friend,

Thank you for having reacted so charitably to my article.[1] You say you're astonished that I set myself to "follow Garaudy to the letter" after having accused him of abusing people's confidence. I followed him, because my article had to do with what he wrote. I didn't follow him "to the letter", because I caught two words, two parenthetical expressions in his text, that I suspect he introduced, in all good faith to be sure, into a citation from Teilhard de Chardin. I say in all good faith, since if Teilhard's text doesn't mean what Garaudy thinks it means, it hardly makes any sense, but I couldn't find it in Teilhard's original[2] and my long habit, as a medievalist, of spotting glosses, made me think the two expressions belonged to Garaudy. Father Philippe de La Trinité[3] wasn't as scrupulous as I am, but anyhow my only infidelity to Garaudy's text is for Teilhard de Chardin's benefit. Nor did I accuse Garaudy of abusing people's trust. What I said was that his book was a political ploy; on that account, everybody should make it his business not to be taken in. Catholics silly enough to believe what he says have only themselves to blame. If the parenthetical expressions are not Teilhard's, Garaudy ought to have put them in brackets, that's all.

The most serious thing is that when I was in Toronto, without the text, I had no means of verifying whether the parenthetical expressions were, or weren't, Teilhard's; and, on second thought, I'm not even sure that Garaudy would have misrepresented his thought if he did slip them in. For Father Teilhard assuredly was no Marxist, since he wasn't an atheist, but I couldn't discuss Garaudy's gloss without mentioning the problem of materialism in Teilhard de Chardin. To say, with Tertullian, that God is a body, is not the same thing as saying there is no God, but without wanting to get into an argument I couldn't get out of, partly through my own fault and partly through his, I wonder if he isn't an advocate of a kind of materialism, as Auguste Comte understood the word, that consists in explaining what is above by what is below.[4] With Teilhard, everything goes up into Christianity, "omne datum optimum *desursum*" is "*descendens* a Patre luminum" (James 1:17).[5] But as far as that goes, Teilhard will always have the upper hand because he's remarkably inconsistent. He's like quick-silver.

I'll gladly accept the pages that either I don't know about or I didn't notice because I'm not concerned with the point where he diverges with Marxism; what would interest me (if Teilhard interested me for himself alone) would be to know whether he expressly and explicitly rejected the Marxist notion that matter is in constant progress because it is constantly evolving. Bergson's creative evolution was a spiritual philosophy calling for an ideal genesis of matter; Bergson was a Plotinian, with the One up above and matter down below. Teilhard is something else entirely, and that's why one shouldn't be surprised that he spoke so little of his illustrious precursor.[6] I would hesitate for a long time, I admit, before I accused Garaudy of abusing our confidence on that score. Teilhard is too changeable for anybody to be able to reproach him even with straight-out materialism, but he's gone about everything in such a way that materialists (Marxists or not) can legitimately claim to draw their inspiration from him.[7]

Further, what bothers me about him has nothing to do with all that. What worries me is rather that while all our Christian theologians, starting with your allegorists, developed their theologies from meditation on the Scriptures, Teilhard, grounded in his evolutionist consciousness, built his theology from a meditation on science. Thus it amazes me when people stick his Pauline sayings about the "cosmic and evolving" Christ up on the bulletin board, because if sin and grace are not the very foundation of the Epistle to the Romans, I don't know anything about Saint Paul. Myself, I'd a hundred times rather be a Lutheran than a Teilhardian. The real Saint Paul is the one whose Christ *tollit peccata mundi*, not the type that would cause a theologian to reject, as the vicious belief that everything has always been the same, the very existence and even the possibility of sin. Whoever does not believe in sin has no right to the Christ Saint Paul believed in. This point is the telling one, because if there's no such thing as sinful nature, then nature is completely good, chastity is a curiosity that should be relegated to an antique shop, etc. What we have here is just plain naturalism.[8] And this is where Garaudy has got it exactly right. This is the bait he will use to catch all the Christians who secretly aspire to appropriate what naturalism calls freedom while still calling themselves Christians. Garaudy makes the most legitimate use of Teilhard;[9] I wish I could, in good conscience, think as much of this man as so many Christian theologians do.

I absolutely loathe this kind of discussion. You can't get any benefit or any enlightenment from thinking about Teilhard. The ravages he has wrought, that I have witnessed, are horrifying. I do everything I can to avoid having to talk about him. People are not content with just teaching him, they preach him; they use him like a seige-engine to undermine the Church from within (I'm not kidding); and I, for one, want no part in this destructive scheme.

But you are right to have faith in my friendship for you, that, I know, is solidly grounded and indestructible. Thank you for being my friend in spite of my rigorous ways which I can understand upset my friends so much!

As ever,

É. GILSON

[1] Gilson is responding to a letter in which, as I thanked him for his book *Les Tribulations de Sophie*, I chided him for having thought he was citing Teilhard by quoting him in Garaudy (on the "Marxist God of the future"), a confusion all the more grave since Garaudy used already outdated texts from Teilhard that concerned something else altogether, to support his Marxist propaganda. The article was written to reproduce a lecture that had been given at the invitation of Monsignor Dino Staffa. I had pointed Gilson's mistake out to him, not without some misgivings.

[2] Gilson had not, at that time, read Teilhard's text (even out of its proper context); still, he went ahead and summarized it in the following paragraph. His embarrassed explanations show that he was justifiably wary of Garaudy—but not wary enough.

[3] Father Philippe de La Trinité, discalced Carmelite (from the Rambaud family from Lyon), then professor in the Carmelite Theological College in Rome, who had started a crusade against Teilhard. In 1964, in *L'Homme devant Dieu* (Aubier), 3:223–248, "La vision religieuse et cosmique de Teilhard de Chardin", Father Gaston Fessard, S.J., rigorously and precisely analyzed the doctrinal presuppositions behind the criticisms Philippe de La Trinité made of Teilhard; but no serious study of this kind seems ever to have fallen into the hands of Gilson (nor of Maritain and several others).

[4] These diverse suspicions (plus an excessive recovery of confidence in Garaudy in the following paragraph) seem to me to be "ramblings", to use Gilson's own word.

[5] Such opposition springs from an obvious error. Whenever it was a question of the Creation, Revelation, the Incarnation, Grace, etc., Teilhard had said over and over again, at every point in his life, exactly what Gilson accuses him of leaving unsaid or even of contradicting. His texts are so clear, so explicit, so insistent, so *coherent*, that it is impossible to make a mistake about them. The word "descent" itself, used to express God's initiative, is familiar to him. He likes to condense Christ's work into these three words from Saint Paul: "*Descendit, ascendit, ut impleret omnia.*" Moreover, if an "upward movement" toward God is possible for every man, for every "soul" (a word dear to Teilhard), it is "solely" because there has already been a "descending movement, a kenosis, a supreme humility" on God's part. The believer's act of faith can be produced only "under the influence of grace". This is a "prevenient grace" which inspires "our first prayer", and all spiritual progress is nothing but a "new response to a new gift". "The attitude that places us securely within the truth is that of the Presentation, in which we expose ourselves humbly to the light of the Infinite shining down on us, with the burning desire that penetrates us and transforms us into himself", etc. The year he died, Teilhard meditated on

Revelation, which is, as he noted down, "The Beyond manifesting itself personally to the here-below". Is that "ascent", or "descent"? See H. de Lubac, "Descente et montée dans l'oeuvre du Père Teilhard", in *Blondel et Teilhard de Chardin* (Beauchesne, 1965).

I have to say it again: such willful misinterpretations are explainable only in the light of a fit, brought on by truly legitimate worry about the "postconciliar" chaos, on top of which came the thrust of Communist propaganda right after the war. Undoubtedly all these things set Gilson up as Teilhard's natural opponent, but there is no excuse for so many mistakes that one just wouldn't expect from a man of Gilson's caliber. On the outer limits of his work, there was an area where he left himself open to being dragged into a war of words without very good reason, at the behest of friends with axes to grind. Having been acquainted with Teilhard *only slightly*, he nonetheless clashed with a posthumous "Teilhardism" zealously pumped out by admirers who were hardly worth knowing and pamphleteers, so it is almost always at second- or third-hand that Gilson speaks. Yet given that he put so much faith in Garaudy, would it be so strange if he put too much faith in such eminent Thomists as Maritain and Cardinal Journet, whose frank hostility to Teilhard, clearly not based on a very well-informed grasp of things, attracted a mixed bag of still less-enlightened hangers-on? (See some details—among others—in the "Témoignage d'un tard-venu à l'Église", by Father Jean-Mohammed Abd el-Jalil, O.F.M., *Cahiers de vie franciscaine* [1967], II: 63–73; reprinted in the "Recueil Jean-Mohammed Abd el-Jalil", *Nouvelles de l'Institut catholique de Paris* 3 (June 1980].) It is sad to note that even on the most critical point under discussion here, where he goes entirely too far, Gilson thought he could make a completely false accusation his own, an accusation brought by two of his friends who were blinded by hatred (I've proved it), when he could have discovered for himself, in Garaudy's own words, that it was wrong. Whatever purpose Garaudy may have had in exploiting the "Teilhardian" fad, in line with the general platform of his party that had drained its whole movement of history in order to succeed in becoming Marxist, and however unable he might have been to enter into Teilhard's spiritual dimension—whence his mangling of the language—Garaudy knew very well that in his "mystical concept of transcendence" Teilhard saw God "at the source of the whole movement" and "the world 'called' from on high" (*Perspective de l'homme* [PUF, 1959], 187–190). Yet he exploited Teilhard just as he exploited the Church's own *Credo*.

[6] Teilhard quotes very little, and he prefers quoting scholars to quoting philosophers. For a comparison with Bergson, see M. Barthélemy-Madaule, *Bergson et Teilhard de Chardin* (Seuil, 1963). (The two men's concepts of evolution, while they do have some points in common, are quite different.) Without trying to compile an exhaustive list, the author noted thirty-four instances where Teilhard has something to say on Bergson.

[7] The blanket charge of "inconsistency" is an *effugium* that can be denied with total justification. Teilhard had a much greater concern for philosophical rigor than people often were willing to grant. And that was taking into account all the different points of view he adopted by turns, and notwithstanding the evolution of thought throughout his writings that spanned nearly half a century, and that he himself points out in various places. He always took good care, whatever people say about him, not to mix up literary genres or academic disciplines. See, for example, his treatise on methodology, "Esquisse d'une dialectique de l'esprit" (1946), in *Oeuvres* (Seuil), 7:147–158.

[8] All that is absurd. "The real Saint Paul" is not found whole and entire just in the Epistle to the Romans, and the real Christ is *also* the one by whom and in whom "*omnia*

*constant*" (cf. a series of texts by exegetes and other Catholic authors who say just what Teilhard said, in *La Prière du Père Teilhard de Chardin,* 45–57). Besides, Teilhard's texts on sin, including original sin, and including the consequences of sin enunciated in the Gospel, are numerous. If one concept appears to contradict another, it is because the author takes a stance appropriate to the genre of any given book, and precisely because he distinguishes very well between the genres, as much from the viewpoint of a social scientist paying attention to the laws of statistics, as from that of personal conscience and faith. Nowhere near plunging us into "plain naturalism", Teilhard was always a strict moralist; for years he criticized the goal of "getting better", to which he opposed "being more". His morality on the subject of marriage is exacting, in advance of, and in full conformity with Paul VI's and John Paul II's calls for a return to the Church's doctrine. He exalted chastity. On his concept of oneness in love, directly inspired by his Marian devotion, see, among others, my study entitled *L'Éternel Féminin,* a commentary on one of Teilhard's poems (Aubier, 2nd ed., 1983). Otherwise, Teilhard never had any plans to give us anything like a *summa theologiae,* as Gilson appears to have supposed when he confronted him with "all our Christian theologians".

On March 1, 1967, Monsignor Bruno de Solages wrote to me: ". . . Attached is a letter from Gilson (quite off the beam!) and the rough draft of my answer. . . ."

[9] Garaudy's work, *De l'anathème au dialogue, un marxiste s'adresse au Concile,* was a propaganda-tool, low-level, nothing but meddling, thundering at "conservatism", "the constraints of the authority-structure", "foot-dragging", stirring up to a fever-pitch the ones who were airing their opinions without the proper competence or the Council's approval, extolling "Christian-Marxist dialogue" for the purpose of building together "the global village", using Pius XII and his encyclical *Afflante* any way he cared to . . . , along with

John XXIII and Paul VI, Teilhard and Dubarle, Gonzalez Ruiz and Karl Rahner. . . . Teilhard had been dead ten years, and Europe was not America; the campaign for things like the "Salzburg Talks" was as nothing compared with the perhaps clumsy but apostolic zeal of the exile from New York with regard to Julian Huxley. Garaudy stole Teilhard's "common city" idea and bent it all out of shape, so that it no longer had the meaning that Teilhard, grown old, severely tried spiritually, unwilling to leave his scholarly scientist-friends with only their miserable dream of "evolutionary Humanism", had originally intended. Having acquired the habit of condensing his thoughts when opposing his ideas to scientific opinions, Teilhard had used a slogan that could have had more than one meaning, especially if one discounts the lengthy reflections he was wont to make before coining phrases. But it never could have had the denotation Garaudy forced upon it. For ages Teilhard had refused to have any more truck with the so-called "common city", had pushed aside the whole connotation of a "heartless, faceless super-society", had condemned "social totalitarianism", etc. His verdict, as he expressed it many times, was clear: "Suspended in the Collective, Humanity, so highly-exalted over the past two centuries, has become a terrifying Moloch" (*L'Atavisme de l'esprit*, 29, etc.).

Quite understandably, considering the spiritual climate of those days, Gilson, having laid siege to Teilhard, tumbled into the moat himself. It is shocking to see him, in the same letter where he's just denounced Garaudy's "political ploy", turning right around and giving him such approval. (He had already mentioned, in *Les Tribulations*, something about "political processes" and the "extreme confusion" he felt in that area, but this didn't stop him from affirming "the basic agreement between Father Teilhard de Chardin's Christianity and Mr. R. Garaudy's Marxism" [p. 128].) I found I was more clearly warned by Garaudy himself. He had sent me his book with its section entitled "The Divine Milieu" claiming to comment upon Teilhard, and I had to respond that not one word from those pages bore the slightest resemblance to what is going on in the authentic *Divine Milieu*.

## 12

6, rue Collet, Vermenton, Yonne

May, 1967

Reverend and dear Father and Colleague,

This probably won't be of any use at all to you, but one never knows! I just thought I'd point out—in the book by Father Hyacinthe-Marie Robillard, O.P., *De l'analogie et du concept d'être* (University of Montreal Press, 1963)—appendix II: "De l'anologie métaphorique en théologie chrétienne", which got me all excited, when I read it for the first time. I think you must already be familiar with it, but I wanted to mention it to you just in case. It presents a framework for the synthesis you could do so well: you already have a complete catalogue of well-defined and very suitable materials.[1]

Please forgive my undoubtedly useless eagerness, but accept it as a special token of friendship.

É. GILSON

[1] Gilson, who had been keeping up with my publications for a long time without my knowing it (cf. L. 6 and Appendix I), had taken an interest in what I had written on the Fathers and the medieval theologians. His penchant for Saint Bonaventure, allied to his Thomism without confusing the two genres, would flare up from time to time. Claudel was delighted, in 1928 when he was in New York, by the chapter on "L'anologie universelle" in his *Philosophie de saint Bonaventure*. Here, Gilson is alluding to the volumes of my *Exégèse médiévale*. See also "Église et Cité de Dieu chez saint Augustin", in *Archives d'histoire doctrinale et littéraire*, année 1953 (1954): 5–23: he supports that with a passage from *Méditation sur l'Église* (cf. 2nd ed., p. 68) in order to illustrate shades of meaning in an assertion from his *Métamorphoses de la Cité de Dieu* and by discussing another interpretation of it by the Rev. Journet.

## 13

6, rue Collet, Vermenton, Yonne

May 16, 1967

Reverend and dear Father and Colleague,

My memory seems to have moved out of my poor head, or rather, it refuses to move back in. "This book you pointed out to me . . .", you wrote me on the 12th; could I ask you again what the title was of the book I was recommending to you?

If it was *La Société de masse et sa culture*,[1] it must be on its way to you, because I just checked my list of "those who sent kind words to the author" and it has been mailed to you. If that's the book, don't bother answering this note: but if not, please remind me of the title of the book in question.

I beg your pardon! While I was writing this, I just remembered!! It was the book by Father Hyacinthe-Marie Robillard, O.P., *De l'anologie et du concept d'être*, appendix II: "De l'analogie métaphorique en théologie chrétienne": symbolic theology and scientific theology, pp. 345–377.

A note to any of your Jesuit colleagues in Montreal would bring you a copy. This Dominican doesn't seem to have heard tell that you are a Jesuit. Anyway, the publisher is University of Montreal Press, C.P. 6128, Montreal 3, Quebec, Canada. And the author quotes Winston Churchill: the Italian campaign "was a dagger-thrust into Germany's soft underbelly", this quote sandwiched between Chenu and Thomas Aquinas, both Dominicans. With friendly greetings, I remain

Respectfully yours,

É. GILSON

[1] In 1967, almost one on top of the other, Gilson sent me two little books: *La Société de masse et sa culture* and *Les Tribulations de Sophie*. In both of them it was a question of new liturgical translations, more especially concerning the *Credo* in the Mass and the Preface of the Holy Trinity. Cf. L. 8, n. 9 and 10. It should be noted that when he speaks of the "liturgical reform", its "authors", or "our liturgical authorities", he is not referring to the work of the Council: he means only the French "translation" of a term of vital importance. To the common-sense objection that could be made to his critique, namely that *substance* is too cultivated a word for the "masses", the "simple believers", he replied with equal, and somewhat mischievous, common sense that "we use symbols not to explain a mystery, but to define it. Now, you don't define it by saying that the Son is of the same

147

nature as the Father, because that is true of all sons. It would be an unfathomable mystery if a son were not of the same nature as his father. By affirming that they are of the same nature, you aren't saying anything, except to declare a truth of the same kind as what made M. de la Palice* famous". Yet one must keep in mind how terribly shaken he was when he saw that "they have cut the word 'consubstantial', that had stood unchanged since the Council of Nicaea ended in 325, as part of the Liturgy in the Creed at Mass and in the Preface of the Holy Trinity, out of the French text; something that, for every Catholic born before the liturgical reform, was inseparable from the very Faith he would rather have died for than deny" (*La Société de masse*, 120, 129). Here, he is by no means criticizing the "new" liturgy's official text; he's defending it.

*[or, M. de la Palisse, character in a French song, noted for his silly sayings—Tr.]

## 14

May 28, 1967[1]

With my heartfelt gratitude for your grand book on the paradox and mystery of the Church.[2] Even a few Teilhardian bugs in the delectable Whole [a pun on one of Teilhard's terms—Tr.] did not succeed in spoiling it for me.[3] Incidentally my friends in Toronto (the Reverend Father Shook) are *delighted* with your note,[4] but they aren't giving me any information about its contents.[5]

Is it possible you've already converted them??[6]

With friendly good wishes, I remain

Respectfully yours,

É. GILSON

[1] During this year, 1967, Gilson was finishing writing *Constantes philosophiques de l'être*, his last work, that was ready for posthumous publication in January 1968 (preface by J.-F. Courtine). In chapter 7, "L'Être et Dieu", he did yet another rewrite job on the theme he had dealt with many times from different angles; a theme I too upheld, constantly enjoying

his friendly good will and support. I have always felt that one or another of the ones he happened to treat harshly would one day come back to him, arriving at unity with his thought by a different approach. I'll excerpt a few of the final lines from this chapter: ". . . The true God himself has to speak to man if he wants his creature to know him. . . . He has allowed man to see him in the person of Jesus Christ. His word has never stopped being reimparted by the Church and articulated with deeper understanding by tradition. . . . The most profound secret of Christian philosophy is perhaps the relationship, at the same time both simple and unfathomable, that Christian philosophy has been bold enough to establish between nature and the supernatural end for which nature is created, although it is impossible for nature naturally to have any inkling of the existence of this relationship, a relationship nature has no natural right to hope for."

[2] *Paradoxe et mystère de l'Église* (Aubier, 1967) that I had told Gilson about in April. The title was borrowed from the first chapter, that reproduced a meditation I had read at an evening gathering during the Notre Dame International Theological Congress (Indiana, USA) in March 1966.

[3] These "bugs" can be found on pages 19, 20, 21, 23, 25, 116, 146, 160.

[4] At the Toronto International Theological Congress (August 20–25, 1967), whose proceedings have been published by Laurence K. Shook, C.S.B., and Guy-M. Bertrand, C.S.C., under the title *La Théologie du renouveau* (Montreal-Paris: Fides-Cerf, 1968). This Congress was held on the hundredth anniversary of the Canadian Confederation. Several of the papers and discussions that followed showed the effects of the "extraordinarily volatile atmosphere" of the time, as noted by the editors.

[5] Vol 2:165–187: "Teilhard de Chardin dans le contexte du renouveau". This is where I cited, toward the end, these words of Teilhard's: "Blessed are we with the authority of

the Church! Left to ourselves, how far off the track would we be in danger of straying?", and another quote that celebrated the "living tradition of the Church, her treasure" that contains "infinitely more truth than all our simplifying philosophies". I went on to cite the three essential points of the Christian Faith threatened by the crisis that raged immediately following the Council, that Teilhard had always portrayed in striking terms: "Faith in a personal God, faith in the divinity of the historical Christ, faith in the reality of the Phylum [i.e., evolving—Tr.] Church"; I then recalled his opposition to the whole idea of a "secular Christianity"; I further underlined his realism, his "sense of being", the "deep love of being" in which he prayed God to keep him always, and that he held in common with the Thomist Gilson (but would Gilson ever have guessed it?).

[6] Gilson had taken part in the Congress, but he had had to leave before the end and didn't get to hear me. Cf. 1:61–62: "Plaidoyer pour la servante" [A Plea for (Philosophy as) the Handmaid [of Theology]—Tr.] (a title taken from a passage from Saint Thomas, *Summa Theologiae, Prima*, q. 1, a. 5: the *doctrina sacra* has the *aliae scientiae* as her handmaids, *ancillae hujus;* allusion to Proverbs 9:3). Cf. H. Gouhier, in his preface to Gilson's *L'Athéisme difficile*, where the "Plaidoyer . . ." is reproduced, pp. 75–95.

## 15

Paris, November 9, 1967

Reverend and dear Father and Friend,

Of course you can write me everything that's on your mind![1]—Otherwise, what kind of friends would we be? Besides, it's quite possible, all too possible, that you are right; my only reason for not being sure of it is the distance that separates what I say from what I think. I say only what seems to me to stand out from the internal evidence. I think what I have to think to make certain texts intelligible, but then one gets into psychology, the least certain of the sciences (if it is one) and into judging consciences, which belongs only to God.[2] Furthermore, I am hoping to get out of these verbal battles, in which I got involved without exercising much caution, I admit. Sometimes one assumes responsibilities that are none of one's business.[3] If there were no laymen, it would be too much fun to be a priest; maybe God wanted to temper the happiness of his *sortiti*[4] [chosen ones—Tr.]! Thank you again. I am

Very affectionately yours,

É. GILSON

[1] I have no recollection whatever of the letter Gilson is answering. Could it have been about Father Teilhard de Chardin again?

[2] Cf. L. 2, n. 3.

[3] Please note the humble frankness of this admission.

[4] See a similar reflection, L. 6, n. 10 and 13.

## 16

6, rue Collet, Vermenton, Yonne

September 3, 1968

Reverend and dear Father and Friend,

Your good letter warmed my heart, because you certainly see the depth of my respect and friendship. Respect cannot diminish this friendship nor can it introduce even a hint of aloofness, depend upon it, and I use the fine old word friendship in its fullest, classical sense: *eadem velle*, etc.

To tell the truth, it puts me in mind of something that's just happened to me: I think a letter I wrote has been sent on to the Vatican and has, at least partially, been made public. I didn't know anything about it. I'm waiting for the rural mail-carrier,* and maybe I'll have the answer in a few minutes, but I can't count on it. So I have to tell you exactly what has been happening.

Jean Guitton published an article in *Le Figaro*, publicly declaring his allegiance to the encyclical letter on the use of artificial contraceptives.[1] This article, whose date and exact wording I've forgotten, was so moving, and expressed my own feelings so well, that I immediately wrote to Jean Guitton to thank him for it, even more than to congratulate him on it.

And then, I receive from the Vatican Secretariat of State a copy of the magnificent Vatican edition of the two Epistles attributed to Peter, with a preface by that same J. Guitton, where I am relieved to find that no one is bound to consider them to be the work of the Prince of the Apostles. But this matter of the authorship of the Epistles has no importance at all and doesn't come into my story. A letter accompanies the shipment. This letter, signed by a Secretary of State whose name I've never been able to decipher, informs me of the Holy Father's pleasure on reading my letter to Jean Guitton, and, adding his pontifical blessing, he presents me with this splendid publication.

That means Jean Guitton must have turned all or part of the letter I had sent to him over to the Holy Father, and I reckon that this is the letter, which started out to be wholly personal, that has just been communicated to the general public. I don't mind at all if either Guitton or the Vatican, to be ·sure, sees fit to do this. I'm perfectly ready to put my name publicly to anything I've signed privately, only the very idea of writing *the Pope***a letter of approbation* (!) seems to me such a lot of nerve, from a layman, that I am afraid people are going to think I've done something totally contrary to the way I characteristically react. It hardly matters; I'm just telling you so you'll be aware of what's going on. Your letter gives you that right.

I've always been very reticent before my betters. I'd never have dared take up a half-hour of Bergson's life just for my own benefit; the only time I had a conversation with him that wasn't accidental was when, at Strasbourg, he invited me to talk with him. I never went to see Claudel, that unique phenomenon in the history of French literature. I often ran into him by chance, and our passing conversations were unforgettable, but I never thought I was important enough to take up five minutes of his time.[2] The thought of paying Paul VI a visit would never enter my head, and maybe that's wrong, because this man of God, endowed with a prophet's soul, as you have said of him with perfect justice,[3] could well be, as much as anyone, in great need of both comfort and simple human affection; and wouldn't comfort and affection help to make up for the indignities with which he is deluged—indignities that even some of his sons shower on him?[4] This is why I think you, since you're a priest, and a priest twice over because you belong to the Society of Jesus, should not hesitate to let him know how you feel. You had (to my knowledge) but one enemy at the Vatican, and he was a Jesuit. Monsignor Montini held you in very high regard, and

I'm sure that esteem can only have increased with the passing years. A priest, a theologian as well known and as universally respected as you are, has no reason to feel the timidity that keeps me, too often perhaps, from telling those I admire most how much I look up to them.[5]

After all, our blessed Lord was not satisfied with just being loved; he keeps wanting people to tell [qu'on le lui *dise* (translator's italics)] him so: "Peter, do you love me?"

Should I have said *dise* or *dît*? The grammar requires *dît*, but what obscure emotion makes me prefer *dise*? I must tell you that I'm almost satisfied with the ending I wrote yesterday to complete a little book on the philosophical constants of language.[6] That must be why I'm beset with grammatical scruples! But because of that, I had the pleasure of rediscovering the stunning pages of Plato's *Seventh Letter contra scripturam*, and of noticing for the first time its disturbing metaphysical significance.[7]

Yes, we do have a prophetic Pope, whose gift of prophecy is so obviously a gift from God that he is bowed down beneath its weight.[8] Everything we can do to help him bear it, let us do. Thank you again for your excellent letter and please be sure that I remain

Your faithful friend,[9]

É. GILSON

157

*The postman came, but I found nothing in the mail, neither letter nor newspaper, concerning this incident. [Gilson's own note, at the foot of this letter—Tr.]

** The words in italics were written by Gilson in red ink.

[1] Paul VI, encyclical *Humanae vitae*, July 25, 1968. This pontifical statement is known to have been poorly received by many, and certain theologians, after the fact, even questioned its canonical validity, arguing that it had failed to be "accepted".

[2] The two examples cited, Bergson and Claudel, well portray the particular admiration Gilson had for both these men.

[3] An allusion to a few pages of my book *Paradoxe et mystère de l'Église*, chap. 5, pp. 168–179: "Paul VI pèlerin de Jérusalem". There I analyzed the essential idea of two of Paul VI's speeches to the Council, given October 28 and December 5, 1963, whose meaning had escaped the press and that did not seem to have been much better understood by the Fathers assembled at the Council (at least the first time they heard them), in spite of the applause they received.

[4] For some especially vicious examples, see *Petite Catéchèse sur nature et grâce*, Communio series (Fayard, 1980), appendix D: "Le 'culte de l'homme', en réparation à Paul VI", pp. 181–200. Cf. André Frossard, in an article published in *Notiziario* 7 (November 1983) (magazine published by l'Instituto Paolo VI, Brescia), pp. 52–54: "None of the Popes that we have seen at work over the past half-century has been more unjustly manhandled and misunderstood. . . . Paul VI, during the entire length of his reign, saw not a single day on which he was not thwarted or contradicted, when people did not hurt his feelings so deeply that it cut him to the heart, when people did not mock or flatly refuse to understand his most forthright aims. . . . How could any generous-hearted man put up with such aggressive opposition for so many years without becoming sadly discouraged and worn out by it all? It was not necessary to be very close

to Paul VI to see that he had hardly any weapon to use against all this ill-will, except the artless kindliness of a heart that was trusting by nature. . . ."

[5] In fact, I saw Paul VI alone only once, in an impromptu audience he himself initiated on the occasion of a meeting of the International Theological Commission, and that hardly lasted ten minutes, when we exchanged but a few cordial although rather commonplace remarks. (Having been prevented from receiving the members of the Commission in a general audience, as he normally would have done, when he learned that I was still in Rome after everyone else had left, the Pope wanted to express to me his appreciation for the whole group's accomplishments.) Was this before or after this letter of Gilson's? I don't remember. In the latter case (which is the more probable), caught unprepared and on the point of leaving Rome, I wouldn't have been able to get together an effective response to Gilson's advice, or more correctly, his urgent appeal, to try to encourage the Pope, that you have just read. I'm all the sorrier, for I had a great many reasons for personally thanking him, both for the encouragement I had received from him, even before he became Pope, and for the votes of confidence he gave me afterward (as his two predecessors had also done in the past). Viewing the matter more objectively, I don't feel quite so bad. To tell the truth, I know perfectly well that there are more important things one can do for a Pope to whom injustice has been done, than just offering him a Veronica's veil of sympathy, as Hans Urs von Balthazar has reminded us (in his well-done chapter "Être pape aujourd'hui" ["The Pope Today"], in his *Points de repère* [*Elucidations*, English translation (London: S.P.C.K., 1975)]. Nevertheless, the more I see of the spiritual ruins heaped up by "loud-mouthed Christians, clergy for the most part, who will not stop wantonly criticizing Rome" and "acting as if they consider themselves angels of truth sent by heaven, by humanity, or by

the future", when they ought to go and "see what they really look like in the pictures of Christ before Pilate by Bosch and Brueghel", the more I regret having forgotten, when it would have been the ideal moment, the appeal Gilson had made to me.

[6] *Linguistique et philosophie. Essai sur les constantes philosophiques du langage* (Vrin, 1969), chapter 7: "La septième lettre", that ends with a quotation from Saint Augustine, *In Joannis ev.* 1, 1, 8: "When thou thinkest these things, it is the Word of God in thine heart."

[7] Cf. ibid., 251, in the note: "What the *Phaedra* and the *Seventh Letter* emphasize is the defenselessness of the written word, that, left all alone, is vulnerable to any kind of misunderstanding on anyone's part, with its author no longer around to protect it. In case of need, a man can explain himself; a book cannot."

[8] Gilson also knew all about the truce—an uneasy truce—in Paul VI's makeup, between the leadings of his heart and the consciousness of his duty to the authority his office had laid upon him. On July 9, 1963, he had written to Father Maurer: "*Habemus Papam!* I know him and I like him. Since they couldn't elect Cardinal Bea, they made what is probably the best choice. I can't keep from smiling when I hear them call him a liberal, whatever they mean by that. Applied to him, they'd have to, somehow or other, make that adjective compatible with the memorable declaration he made to me one day: 'What authority means is not to have to give reasons'" (Shook, *Gilson*, 365). Cf. L. 17, n. 4. Paul VI really had a lofty conception of papal authority, "the power of fatherhood, of service, of salvation. . . . It comes from Christ. . . . Whoever opposes this institution that embodies the apostolic power of sanctification, of teaching, of governing, will pit himself against the word, against the plan, against the love of Christ" (public audience, November 4, 1964). Beginning with his first encyclical, *Ecclesiam suam* (August 6, 1964),

he insisted on various occasions on this "supreme authority", that comes "not from spiritual pride and the human will to dominate", but "from service and from love" (*Acta Apostolicae Sedis,* 1964: 611–614, 617, 656–659). Notice especially the following passage (p. 622): "In this encyclical Letter We are purposely abstaining from setting forth any opinion whatsoever on the subject of the principal points of doctrine concerning the Church, which have already been proposed for the consideration of the Ecumenical Council over which We preside. In truth, for the moment, We wish that this assembly, so distinguished and of such authority, enjoy full freedom of research and of discussion, reserving to Our apostolic office of Teacher and Pastor placed at the head of the Church of God the choice of the proper time and manner to express Our thought: then, nothing will be more desirable to Us than to be able to present it in perfect concord with the judgment of the Fathers of this Council." As Cardinal Montini, he had written, in the autumn of 1962, to Cardinal Cicognani, then president of the General Commission of the Council: "The Church rejoices in recognizing in Peter and his successor this fullness of powers that are the secret of her unity, of her strength. Why do you not say this? . . ."

[9] This letter shows at once Étienne Gilson's modesty, his deep-rooted sensitivity, his vital Catholic awareness—and no less the acute pain from the wound that the Church's troubles caused him in the days immediately following the Council.

One can read numerous publications on Paul VI put out by the Istituto Paolo VI (Brescia), notably the bi-annual periodical *Notiziario* and the series *Quaderni dell'Istituto* (volume 3 gives the *Discorsi e Scritti nel Concilio*). See also *Paul VI et la modernité dans l'Église*, proceedings of a colloquium organized by l'École française de Rome (Palais Farnèse), 875 pages.

## 17

Paris, September 26, 1969

Reverend and dear Father and Friend,

I am often tempted to think that private citizens—
especially laymen—can't do anything more in the
present circumstances,[1] but you are a priest and
a theologian, and your admirable book goes
straight to the heart of the question of questions,
or rather, straight to the affirmation that is at the
heart of every one of our answers.[2]

What a joy for me to feel so completely at one
with you in heart and mind! And besides, I have
a personal need to be brought back, in this way,
to what I myself think, namely, that becoming
used to words tends to make us forget. Even a
Thomist is in danger of taking the equivalent
(pseudo-equivalent) meanings of πίστις [belief]
and δόξα [opinion] literally, as if the Faith were
a sort of opinion, a δόξα μετά. Your whole book
combats this error and maintains the uniquely
specific quality of the Christian Faith, the first
sign in ourselves of the life of blessedness. I hope
that some will understand you. In any case, you

couldn't have done anything better or more appropriate to persuade your readers of this primary Christian truth: the meaning of the word *Credo*.[3]

> Thank you with all my heart,
> and believe me, I remain
> Your faithful friend indeed,

É. GILSON

P.S. My *other friend*, dear Father M. D. Chenu,[4] is not doing well; he's not happy right now . . .

---

[1] An echo of his disappointment at not having been understood in his request for the restoration of the word "consubstantial" (cf. L. 8, n. 9)—but more still of his sorrow at seeing the disorders of every kind that had been rife for some years now. It was not merely as an intellectual or as an author that Gilson conscientiously fulfilled, at every opportunity, his layman's role. That summer of 1969 he took his parish priest's place preaching the Sunday homilies, while the priest went away for "recycling" [the amusing French term for "continuing education"—Tr.]. See the account he gives of this experience in Shook, *Gilson*, 382–383.

[2] *La Foi chrétienne, essai sur la structure du Symbole des Apôtres* (Aubier, 1969; 2nd ed., 1970).

[3] Among many other signs, this letter sheds light on the depth of Gilson's Catholic Faith. Hating (perhaps a bit too much) everything to do with "apologetics", punctiliously

abiding by the rules and conventions of scholarly research, a stranger to cliques, allergic to clerical snobs, he nonetheless took his share, often an active one, in the labors and hopes of the Church of his time. In the Church's testing-time, he was a faithful member among all the faithful. On November 22, 1979, M. Henri Gouhier recalled, in his speech on being received into the Académie française, a meaningful anecdote that dates from the earliest part of his writing career. A "Note à propos d'Études médiévales" appeared in *La Vie Catholique*, October 25, 1921: "In the note, a clerical watchdog very briefly recognized M. Gilson's abilities, 'but', he added, however, 'let us not be duped! The professor admires church architecture; at times, he allows himself to be moved by sacred music . . . , but he will always remain an *outsider*. . . .'" This last word, in italics, justified everyone's suspicions: people were then picking out a fine collection of virtual heresies in the "professor's" books, with this prudent conclusion: "M. Gilson is a very distinguished scholar; but you have to know whom you can trust." In the November 1 issue of *La Vie Catholique*, Étienne Gilson's response bore the title: "Pour travailler tranquille". He corrected an over-hasty reader's misinterpretation, and then he made an astute comment on the italicized word, "outsider": "Might I know, an outsider to what?" he asked. "If he considers me an outsider to the Church, he is mistaken, since I was brought up in the Catholic Faith and I profess it explicitly. . . . If he is just putting me out of his party, undoubtedly he has his reasons: however, I can tell him that mine remains open to him, and its patrons are Saint Francis and Saint Dominic."

[4]On Father M. D. Chenu, O.P. (born in 1895), there is a note (going up to 1950) by G. Jacquemet in *Catholicisme* (Letouzey et Ané), vol. 2: col. 1041–1042. After his studies in Rome, he taught from 1920 to 1942 at the "Studium" at Saulchoir (in Belgium, then at Étoiles), where he was regent. Between 1959 and 1978, he co-directed the *Archives d'histoire*

*doctrinale et littéraire du Moyen Age* with Gilson. In 1937, Father Chenu had written a little book: *Une école de théologie, le Saulchoir*, that was printed, but not sold commercially—and put on the Index in February 1942. That year, the Master-General (Gillet) sent Father Garrigou-Lagrange (cf. L. 9, n. 8) to France as apostolic visitor to monastic houses of study and publishing centers. He, in turn, stuck in the Southern Zone by the "line of demarcation", had to be replaced in the "Occupied Zone" by Father Thomas Philippe. After the war, Gilson had an audience in Rome with Monsignor Montini; he told him he had found in his friend's little book only three doctrinal conclusions, and, after having shown him what they were, asked him to tell him which of them was inconsistent with Catholic doctrine. That was when Montini answered Gilson with the scintillating response noted above, L. 16, n. 8. "His French", said Gilson, "was impeccable" (cf. Shook, *Gilson*, 248). In another set of circumstances, Father Chenu showed a similar generosity; back in 1935 he had protested the "calumnies" to which Blondel was in danger of falling victim (cf. Blondel and Valensin, *Correspondance* 3:187). In 1946 the Toronto Institute tried to offer him a teaching post; but when authorization was sought through the mediation of Maritain, the new ambassador to the Vatican, it was refused by the competent Congregation (Pizzardo).

The little book on Le Saulchoir was first reprinted in an Italian translation (Marietti, 1982), and then in French (Cerf, 1985), with studies by Giuseppe Alberigo, Étienne Fouilloux, Jean Ladrière, and Jean-Pierre Jossua; with a preface by René Rémond.

## 18

6, rue Collet, Vermenton, Yonne

about 1971 (?)

Thank you, Reverend Father, for your good letter. Language, today, is not of primary concern to the French Catholic.[1] We can't be certain whether we're in communion with our bishops. I can't keep from suspecting that the priest who patently garbles the Consecration at the Sunday Eucharistic Assembly still thinks his sloppy commemoration effects the transubstantiation.[2] It's sad, and there's nothing I can teach you on that score, but it's wormwood and gall to me, and at least I can tell you about it and feel reasonably sure it's the same for both of us. That's a consolation.[3]

Very faithfully yours,

É. GILSON

[1] Gilson is answering a letter I had written to thank him for his work *Linguistique et philosophie* (end of 1969). These gruff remarks express the ever-present heaviness of heart that darkened his last years. Even in 1967, the final chapter of *Les Tribulations de Sophie* was entitled "Divagations parmi les ruines". In it he pointed out the "generalized tendency to obliterate the distinction between clergy and laity, a minor symptom of a growing pressure to take the character of holiness out of religion"; a tendency that was only accentuated in the years that followed, inspiring a series of publications that shamelessly falsified Church history.

[2] Formed in the heat of emotion, the sentence seems to me to have been poorly phrased; but the general idea is clear. It was already there for anyone to read in *Les Tribulations de Sophie*, 142: "The ideas are more arcane than the rites. . . . Undoubtedly the most troubling puzzle for the laity could be these ideas, that the priest keeps hidden in his head, that chart his conduct for him, but that the faithful cannot know."

[3] It is certainly regrettable that, in certain of his later writings, Gilson may have mixed really pertinent remarks with one or two curmudgeonly traits that make one think of an elderly parishioner with eccentric ways; and this can give people an excuse not to listen to him. He was suffering because he could no longer speak frankly with his Church's legitimate representatives, so effectively had the myth of the "renewed Church" blinded many pastors to reality, or at least influenced their attitudes and their way of speaking. But Gilson found refuge, and a very real consolation that transcended his anguish, in the Holy Scriptures. Cf. the vignette that Father Jacques-Guy Bourgerol, O.F.M., recounts in *Étienne Gilson et nous: la philosophie et son histoire* (Vrin, 1980), 42: "As he handed me the manuscript, difficult to read because of many erasures, of the introduction to the Centenary Book *Saint Bonaventure 1274–1974*, he told me on the morning of

November 17, 1972, in his study in the rue Saint-Romain in Paris: 'My dear Father, as of now I have only one book left in my library, the Bible.'"

## 19

89460 Cravant

Tuesday, July 1, 1975

Reverend and dear Father,

I was deeply touched by your good letter. Don't think I've ever failed to appreciate, much less been indifferent to, your affection.

If it had been up to me, you would have succeeded Father Daniélou[1] as a member of the Académie Française.

I know it would be useless to discuss it with you.

The confused situation that Father Carré's election resolved confirms my hunch that I did right to abstain.

Besides, that's of no importance at all, but brotherly love like yours, and the prayers it inspires in you, are very precious to me.

Please accept, Reverend and dear Father, the assurance of my respect and devoted friendship.

for ÉTIENNE GILSON[2]

[1]Jean, Cardinal Daniélou, S.J., had died May 20, 1974, worn out before his time by a life of hard work and by a wide-ranging apostolate, a life wholly dedicated to the service of the gospel. Several of the architects, or followers, of what Paul VI defined as the "self-destruction of the Church" (even within the family of Father Daniélou's own Jesuit Order) relentlessly tried to ruin him. He let himself be neither intimidated nor embittered in the least. His spiritual influence was profound. His first work, *Le Signe du Temple*, was in every way a masterpiece; later on, outside of his scientific work, he gave up more and more of his literary activities to make room for his consuming dedication to his ministry. The issues of the *Bulletin des amis du cardinal Daniélou* printed between 1975 and 1985 contain numerous documents about him and his work (Société des amis du cardinal Daniélou, 24, boulevard Victor-Hugo, 92200 Neuilly-sur-Seine).

[2]Étienne Gilson died on September 20, 1978, at Cravant (in the vicinity of Auxerre). In 1974, his friends had given him, in celebration of his ninetieth birthday, his last book: a collection of his studies on *Dante et Béatrice*. On April 8, 1975, Paul VI had sent him a long "autograph" letter, as a mark of the gratitude of the whole Church. On the evening of June 18, 1984, on the initiative of Mlle. Marie-Thérèse d'Alverny, who was Gilson's student at Strasbourg in 1920 and who had been closely associated with both Gilson and Father Chenu in their great undertaking in the study of the history of medieval thought, an anniversary Mass was celebrated in Paris at the Dominican Convent of Saint-Jacques. Father Chenou chose the texts for the Epistle (the praise of Wisdom) and the Gospel (the Beatitudes): the first, in remembrance of the wisdom of Saint Augustine preserved as a sacred trust by Saint Thomas and his disciple; the second, to call to mind the evangelical renewal that gave birth to the two Orders of Saint Dominic and Saint Francis. He spoke of this marriage of wisdom and evangelism, that Gilson so admired

and brought to fulfillment by means of a doctrinal synthesis of both. Despite his personal choice of Thomism, the great historian of medieval thought, he told us, was so steeped in the spirit of Saint Bonaventure that, after having finished his commentary on his work, he fell to his knees to adore the Lord and to plead for his mercy. Father Chenu, deeply moved, then described the divergent paths the two friends had taken over the past few years. In fact, he concluded, their disagreeing did not spoil their fundamental unity, because while they saw things differently they never ceased to meet regularly as faithful friends. Cf. Marie-Thérèse d'Alverny and M. D. Chenu, "*In memoriam* É. Gilson", in *Archives d'histoire* 45 (1978): i–iv.

# APPENDICES

# APPENDIX I

## A LETTER FROM
## ÉTIENNE GILSON TO X

Paris, December 25, 1945

Dear Sir,

My grateful thanks for having sent the *Proudhon* by Father Henri de Lubac.[1] I have just read it with the greatest interest and I consider it the best introduction we possess in French to Proudhon's work.

Please be kind enough to convey my sincere congratulations to the author of this fine book, and please accept my very best regards.

É. GILSON

[1] Through whose good offices did I acquire this letter? I no longer have any memory of it. Undoubtedly it must have been sent to me (as Gilson asked him to do) by Emmanuel

Mounier, director of the "La condition humaine" collection in which this *Proudhon* appeared, published by Éditions du Seuil, in 1945. This was one of three collections that Mounier had set up as a project during the German occupation, and that he wanted to publish as soon as possible, under the marginal sponsorship of the revived magazine *Esprit*. His cheerful bullying had made me compile this work too quickly, using the notes from a course given in the department of theology at Lyon in 1941–1942, that he, happening to live in Lyon, audited in his spare time, sometimes bringing with him Albert Béguin. Busy with other tasks, I never got around to doing a second edition, but Monsignor Pierre Haubtmann, with whom I have had lengthy discussions on Proudhon, has done an infinitely better job with his books.

# APPENDIX II

# IN COMPANY WITH
# FATHER DE LUBAC:
# FAITH SEEKING UNDERSTANDING

I remember the day I found myself with some time on my hands in the library of a Dominican Friary, and what better place is there than the library of a religious house? My eyes chanced to fall upon a book that had lost its binding, worn from being read over and over again, entitled *Surnaturel* and bearing the name of the Reverend Father Henri de Lubac, S.J. Curious, I picked it up, because I had never read it, but I'd often heard it discussed in the tone theologians take when they are advising a prospective reader that he will do well to exercise caution. In short, something like the Censors' film catalogues, a book "strictly for adults". How could it have come about that this rather disquieting book had such well-thumbed pages?

Years have gone by. Father de Lubac's book

has become two books: *Augustinisme et théologie moderne*, and *Le Mystère du surnaturel*.* Here they are on my table, I've just read them, I've been invited to inform the public of their existence and I think so highly of them that something inside of me tells me it's my duty to accept that invitation. Not without scruples, however, for how am I to go about it?

Their two titles alone give some information about the author and his way of thinking. We are inundated with books whose titles are attractive, that promise much and don't keep their promises. Here, on the contrary, are two austere titles to introduce an impassioned work that includes all of the substance of *Surnaturel*, but enriched, matured, brought right up to the minute, and topped off with a refreshing fillip of that quiet satisfaction that characterizes every brilliant man when he finds, at last, that he was the one who had it right all along!

The two-in-one subject of this work is at the very heart of the Christian religion: the relationship between nature and grace, and then the mystery of man's supernatural calling and the economy of revelation, redemption, and, in a word, salvation. Some people say that we need not concern ourselves with speculating on these matters and that we'll get along well enough with ordinary piety. I'd feel tempted to say they were right, as long as they, by being silent, didn't start speculating themselves. It is appalling what can happen to a sound religion when it can't come to an agreement on what its own piety is. A primary virtue of these two volumes is that they make it clear to a lot of people how impossible it is for anyone to turn himself into a theologian all by himself.

Father de Lubac's extraordinary erudition, so often demonstrated in other disciplines, occupies itself here with controversies going back to the time of Saint Augustine and Saint Thomas and reaching even to our own day, controversies that have put so many fine minds at odds on a problem that really ought to be quite simple, given that every Christian's personal life is supposed to be practically settled. But no, ideas and men are forever playing seesaw, continually teetering; now nature is up, now grace, with everybody all the while accusing everybody else of misunderstanding nature's just prerogatives, or alternatively, of encroaching upon rights that belong to God.

This is certainly what Father de Lubac thinks, that everyone is forgetting to notice how these disputes all must eventually collide with mystery. The creation is a mystery. For us, the first of mysteries and the seed of all the others is that God freely created finite being, unable to exist without him; yet, he can subsist, himself, without it, as indeed he has done from all eternity, before ever he made anything that was made. Nature is not grace, but God's free gift of existence is a mystery whose cloud human reason instinctively would like to pierce. Why this gift? Why this act? Could not God foresee man's sin, or even prevent it? Now that the evil has been done, where do we stand with God, and how do we face the problem of sin? What I have called Father de Lubac's erudition astounds me less in its extent than it does in the way it works. He does not muster up theologies for us, but theologians, men like us, whose problems are the same as ours, men we can identify with even in their failures.

Because the problem is our destiny, it carries the same urgency today as ever it did, but those who read these two fine books will soon see that their author would not have written them if he didn't believe that our own time offers a promising opportunity to move the discussion forward. For anyone who has studied history, nineteen centuries of arguing constitute a perspective from which it ought to be easier to determine the true stakes in the debate.

I don't want to distort Father de Lubac's thought by presenting as the guiding principle of his work the dominant impression I have gained from the thrill of reading it, but I do see in it two great figures that stand out, two great saints who were at the same time two great theologians, Saint Augustine and Saint Thomas Aquinas.[1] Neither of them is primarily concerned with theology, but rather with the unfathomable mystery of man, of God, and of the relationship of man to God. Real theologians build their doctrines as explanations of the highest reality, that is, divine reality. Since divine reality is so far beyond them, they don't leave a finished interpretation of it, frozen once and for all in definitive formulae. Their disciples use these great theologies themselves as the object of their reflections, instead of the One the great theologies are all about. Clinging to their formulae rather than to reality, the disciples are amazed to discover that their formulae are not in perfect accord, they try to make them agree, sacrificing, if they have to, certain essential doctrinal aspects in order to force their doctrine into consistency with itself, as if the important thing about doctrine were not that it must first agree with reality. Thus the object is lost from sight, drowned in its own explanation.

Schools of thought in theology, along with their interminable disputes, come into being in this fashion. Father de Lubac's considered opinion, to my mind right on the mark, is that the closer one gets to the source of the great theological movements, the more one notices how they grow together, for the simple reason that they come into contact with theological reality itself, a reality that is one, as opposed to the multiplicity of that reality's expressions.[2]

By calling attention to this return to the sources,

and by standing outside the "falsifying" interpretations that turned Saint Augustine's elegant system into Jansen's mutant that shied away from nature, and Thomism into the Aristotelian naturalism that hid itself from grace, Father de Lubac is not unaware that the necessity of such problem-solving is renewing in itself: "The naturalist bypath Baius cut to lead people off the main road, the detour that has taken so many twists and turns since the sixteenth century, makes it our duty to go forward theologically. It beckons us to a new effort to think things through. Now, more than ever, the gratuity of the supernatural must be clearly drawn and fully explained; we have to learn where the signposts are and work out a more rational plan for getting there." The great lesson this book teaches, a lesson as true as it is fascinating, is that if theological progress is sometimes necessary, it is never possible unless you go back to the beginning and start over. Father de Lubac's two volumes will be a priceless help to those of us who are doing our best to get back to the Way.

É. GILSON, of l'Académie française
*La Croix*, July 18–19, 1965

* Two octavo volumes of 333 and 300 pages respectively (Théologie Series, nos. 63 and 64 [Paris: Aubier, 1965]).

Actually, the first volume was an enlarged second edition of the first part of the book *Surnaturel,* and the second was an amplification of a 1949 article on "Le mystère du Surnaturel".

[1]The connection that Gilson, unlike most of the "Thomists" and "Augustinians" of his day, made between Augustine and Thomas, will be more easily understood in the light of what he wrote back in 1926 in the *Archives d'histoire doctrinale et littéraire du Moyen Age,* vol. 1, "Pourquoi saint Thomas a critiqué saint Augustin": "Having freed Saint Augustine from Avicenna's vise-like grip, Saint Thomas was to prove true the impression that he was not so far removed from the real thought of Saint Augustine as he was from that of his own contemporaries. A God who could be both himself and at the same time our own intellect is radically unacceptable in Thomism; a God who illuminates our intellect without doing our thinking for us, and who consequently acts in our behalf without fusing himself with us is not in any way impossible for Thomism to embrace, and this God is basically the true one besides. Now, this is precisely what Saint Augustine's texts suggested to Saint Thomas: a doctrine of divine illumination, without a set technical definition as to exactly how this illumination operates. . . . Nowhere does Saint Thomas undertake a systematic analysis of Saint Augustine's doctrine, . . . he seems to mention it by accident, rather more to reach out and touch it than to judge it; and the difference there is that, with complete respect for Saint Augustine's recognized authority, he is only criticizing a contemporary fad for 'using Saint Augustine as a tool to teach Avicenna'" (pp. 117–119).

Four years later, in a larger perspective, Gilson made a case for taking Saint Augustine's thought down from the shelf and putting it to immediate and permanent use. "L'avenir de la métaphysique augustinienne", *Revue de philosophie* 2 (1930): 691: "What characterizes Saint Augustine's philosophy is that, for him, revelation is the source, the rule, and even the food of rational thought; he believes faith is the mother of reason and that dogma, taken as such, is the father of philosophy. This does not imply in any way that he mixes belief with knowledge. . . . But what he always wanted to do and succeeded wonderfully in accomplishing was to build, under the guidance of a supernatural light . . ., a system of ideas that, although they were in essence purely rational, would however have been impossible without that light. . . . *Nisi credideritis non intelligetis* [Unless you believe, you shall not know] is now and ever shall be the charter of all Christian philosophy. . . ."

Gilson then rose up against "the suspicions and the species of disfavor that, in the minds of many Catholic thinkers, had kept Saint Augustine out of action as a philosopher", causing an "interior shredding" of Christian thought, whose "indivisible unity", however, "those who live it experience daily". To remedy this situation, some Thomists, for all that they clutched Saint Augustine fiercely to their breasts, succeeded only in skewing Thomism, so that all the Augustinians could do was protest. . . . What is needed is for "those who have exiled themselves from Saint Augustine to come back to him: they will find him right where he has always been, at the center of Christian thought, next to Saint Thomas Aquinas, who may have differed with him but who never separated himself from him (pp. 692–709). While for Maritain Thomism is, in the last analysis, the scientific state of Augustinian wisdom, a scientific state that with Saint Augustine would be "still in embryo", for Gilson "this whole enormous field of interior observation, where he remains unrivalled, would be left to lie fallow if everyone forsook Saint Augustine . . .; the heavenward steps that God has prepared for man's heart would cease to be an object for meditation for the philosopher as such; some of the possible avenues to God would be firmly shut, ways that it would perhaps be better to leave open for the greater benefit of Christian philosophy" (pp. 711–712; cf. J. Maritain, ibid., 737).

[2]On the "theologies other than Thomism", theologies "whose orthodoxy, however, is unquestionable", Gilson wrote two years later (*Les Tribulations de Sophie*, 41): "Each of them seems to me to be called by God to point out an important, indeed vital, stage in the totality of truth. Saint Augustine and his dialectic of time and truth; Saint Gregory of Nyssa, Denis [Pseudo-Dionysius—Tr.] and their apophatic theology; Saint Anselm and his unflagging confidence in the necessity of right reason; Saint Bonaventure, whose metaphysical meditation reaches with unique ease the level of mystical contemplation; the blessed John Duns Scotus and his metaphysic of essences that expands so smoothly into a theology of infinite being (etc.) . . ., all the truth in all of them . . . cannot touch the word of God on which it wants only to be the commentary, the elucidation, and something like an entry-point." He added, "The statement is as valid for Thomas Aquinas as it is for the others", but with this proviso: "The enormous difference I find between him and the others, is that he always lets me understand the truth of their individual theologies, and consequently connect theirs with his, while their theologies do not permit me to understand his. . . ." Perhaps his proviso restricted, even in principle, the extent of the connection. Nevertheless, he "preached peace", even if, as happens to us all, he did not always understand clearly, and consequently was occasionally unable to corral very efficiently the kinds of thought that pulled him off the track. See Appendix V.

# APPENDIX III

## SEVEN LETTERS FROM ÉTIENNE GILSON'S FRIEND FATHER GERALD SMITH, S.J.[1] TO FATHER HENRI DE LUBAC

I

Marquette University, Milwaukee

September 29, 1947

. . . I'm going to tell you about a frustrating thing that happened to me, that has left me somewhat less than enthusiastic about trying to publish books.

After theology, they put me to teaching moral philosophy. I soon discovered that, without metaphysics, moral philosophy doesn't exist. Further, without history, metaphysics is just about incomprehensible. So, about forty years ago, I started studying history under Messrs. Gilson, Maritain, and the Rev. Phelan at the Institute of Mediaeval Studies at the University of Toronto in Canada, where after two years I finally got my doctorate. My dissertation was "Liberty in Molina". The Rev. Phelan, who was then president of the Institute, and M. Gilson pushed me to submit my dissertation to the judgment of the Society of Jesus, telling me it ought to be published.[2] Knowing full well that the dissertation would never pass the censors, because it took a stand against Molina (as it did against Bañez besides), I submitted it anyway, as I didn't want to look as if I were being stubborn in the face of the urgings of professors in the University. Fine. Just as I thought, the censors rejected the dissertation because it took a position on a *non libera* question (see *Epitome*, 317).[3] When the Provincial asked me if I accepted the censure, I said of course, I'm a Jesuit. But, I added, you ought not to be satisfied with it, given that three persons of the standing of Gilson, Maritain, and Phelan approved the book and urged me to publish it. It really looked as if, in view of the rule (*Epit.*, 315, 316) commending Saint Thomas' doctrine, a rule followed immediately by another rule that forbids us to have anything to do with questions *de futuris contingentibus et de scientia media* (*Epit.*, 317), it seemed to me, as I say, that there was a contradiction there somewhere. Because if Molina is right, the rule about Saint Thomas seems hypocritical, since it doesn't mean anything; or, on the other hand, if Saint Thomas is right, the rule about "our" doctrine is useless. When you add it all up, with these *two* rules, we look as if we are legislating either hypocritically or to no purpose. Well, that's the way things have been, lo, these thirty years.

So you can see why I have been more than hesitant to start all this business up all over again by submitting more books just to get more rejections. . . .

<hr>

[1] Father Gerald Smith had studied theology in the French Scholasticate in the Order's provinces of Lyon and Paris, then at Ore Place, Hastings (Sussex, England), and finally at Lyon-Fourvière.

[2] Cf. Gilson's L. 9.

[3] A certain Suarezian and Molinist orthodoxy was formerly required of future teachers in the Scholasticate, at least in a few of the Order's provinces. However, starting in the twenties, the situation had begun to change. From 1920–1923, two of our professors on Jersey, Fathers Pedro Descoqs and Gabriel Picard, the rector, were savage Suarezians. (A third, Father Camille Bonnet, fearing that the young students would go wild when they encountered more subtle doctrines, cheerfully boomed one day: "What our students need, is a good Suarezian soup.") About 1950, the freedom to follow the Suarezian interpretation of Saint Thomas was even demanded in some quarters within the Order (but for a long time without success), against the abusive dominance of a "Thomist" school that was then in power. At the time it was much less a matter of Suarez himself than of a principle of theological liberty within the same Faith. Gilson became an advocate of this needed pluralism, consistent with the Church's tradition, at the Thomist Congress in Rome in 1950.

## 2

Marquette University
Johnston Hall
Milwaukee 3, Wisconsin

January 6, 1949

Dear Father de Lubac, Christ's Peace!

I've just this minute finished reading your article on the *Mystère du surnaturel*.[1] Thank you very much for sending it to me. It is exactly what I was hoping to see: an answer to the critics that gets to the root of the question and in my opinion does an excellent job of it. As for the "supernatural" problem itself, in this case I think you are absolutely right.

The meeting in Boston[2] went very well. As I told you, I was the one who presented the objection (purposely, with a bit of a strategic goal, to see our "enemies" satisfied that we'd treated them right). Dr. A. Pegis responded. But he was speaking only for himself. . . . The result, in my view, was that philosophy in the United States got a forward push. I'm sure people could tell I didn't believe a word of the objections I was making, but they certainly were left with no chance to accuse me of not having presented the case *contra*. Then, when Pegis took your part, the objectors were without a leg to stand on. At least, that's the impression I got. . . .

I suppose, unfortunately, that you haven't yet decided to come over here. Why deny *our* doctors the chance to make some progress? I am persuaded that a change of air would do you good.

My best wishes to everybody at Fourvière. They do some first-rate work.

*In Domino,*

GERRY, S.J.

[1] Article published in 1949 in *Recherches de science religieuse*, pp. 80–121.
[2] Convention of the Catholic Philosophical Society of the United States.

## 3

Milwaukee, December 11, 1950

My dear Father Henri,

Just a little note you don't have to answer. I consider Father X's[1] criticisms (1) revolting (even if
he had been right); (2) unintelligent, seeing that
there's nothing so difficult about understanding
the sovereignty of God if only one looks at it from
God's point of view and not from that of contin-
gent objects. Pegis thinks the same.[2]

Gilson has just given us a lecture: "Les recherches philosophiques et l'avenir du scolas-
ticisme". It was excellent. He maintained that
Scholasticism won't have a future if it isn't supported by the same cause that gave it life: theology.[3] As for the Thomists Garrigou, Boyer, etc.,
he said, in short: they're crazy, the lot of them;
definitely certifiable. "I'm just waiting", he added,
"for the commentary they've promised on the
encyclical; I couldn't comment on the encyclical
itself without being embarrassed, but the commentary! You bet I'll comment on that blasted
commentary!"[4] Great guy, that Gilson. You'll

have to meet him. He considers you one of the most powerful forces in Europe—for the good, and he's not afraid to say so. . . .

[1] He's talking about an American Jesuit professor who zealously duplicated, in his courses and publications, criticisms others had formulated; he had his students regurgitate them in papers on my "heresies" (including "Gallicanism").

[2] Cf. Smith's L. 5 and 6.

[3] Cf. Gilson, *Philosophe et théologie*, chapter 9, "La philosophie chrétienne", pp. 191–216: "As it is defined in the encyclical *Aeterni patris* [Leo XIII, 1879], Christian philosophy is, then, the use the Christian makes of philosophical speculation in his effort to enter into the mind of his Faith, as much in matters accessible to natural reason as in those that are beyond it." End of chapter 10, "L'art d'être thomiste", 232: ". . . To philosophize, as only a Christian can do, *in* the Faith." Cf. pp. 246 and 256.

[4] The fact is that the tenor of a part of the encyclical *Humani generis* (August 1950) had disappointed, and more than disappointed, a number of those who had looked forward to it (for want of something better, people sometimes said) and who had perhaps participated in its production. Two or three of its most ardent promoters were stupefied to find themselves its targets. To add insult to injury, at least two of the doctrines that had been denounced with more bitterness than anyone could imagine over the past several years, got off scot free. Surely, the encyclical must have been carefully checked before publication by people who knew what was what. Up to this very moment, to my knowledge, there still is no truly objective commentary, and no more is there a

factual analysis of Pius XII's attitude toward the situation—an attitude very different, as I learned a little later, than was generally assumed.

## 4

Marquette University

December 31, 1950

. . . Gilson knew very well that you were sitting in on his classes and he wanted to meet you too, but I think that despite his "rough ways" he's just a bit shy. However, he'd be very glad to get to know you. It's true that he won't be back in France until spring and maybe still later than that—on account of the political situation. But when he does return, he'll keep you in stitches with his stories about what went on in Rome.[1] As you know, he gave a lecture at the Thomist Congress in Rome in the month of September. After a talk he gave for us here on December 11, I told him he ought to set all his investigations into the *esse* aside for now and take the time, finally, to do justice to the Essence. After a few stiff shots of our *bourbon*, and because he's a good friend, he told me everything he had on his mind. I gave Father Rondet[2] a few excerpts from what he said to me, and you can ask him to let you see them whenever you like. He told me those things in confidence, but you'll be the soul of discretion.[3] Anyhow, Gilson knows exactly how far to go. He's an extraordinary man: a Thomist without being one, a bit like the way Saint Francis wasn't a hundred-percent Franciscan, a man of good sense, very wise, above cliques, totally fair, and a profoundly holy person. He has always impressed me more than Maritain does, even though I like Maritain very much too.

Try to forget X. He can never be straightened out.[4] Sometimes I ask myself where we stand in theology in the United States. People here go so far as to claim that we've never yet made a false step in theology; maybe that's because we haven't yet made a step. . . .

[1] This was mainly about the repercussions surrounding the encyclical *Humani generis* and various incidents at the Thomist Congress in September. See L. 9, notes 7, 9, 12.

[2] Then professor of dogmatic theology and prefect of studies (since 1948) in the Scholasticate at Fourvière. In the summer of 1951 he became Superior at Grenoble, then at Toulouse and Lyon. He died in 1979. In what has been called the "Fourvière affair", he behaved with perfect rectitude and obedience, never giving in to plotting or other unseemly power-plays. His thesis on the idea of the supernatural in the sixteenth century had been sponsored by Father Charles Boyer.

[3] I didn't save these "confidential accounts", but I received information from other sources.

[4] Cf. Smith's L. 3, n. 1.

## 5

Marquette University
Milwaukee 3, Wisconsin

February 1, 1961

Dear Father Henri,

Delighted to hear news of you! When Father Rondet couldn't tell me anything, we both figured
you were still alive. All these books! And the last
one, *L'Exégèse médiévale*, is a jewel. Make sure the
*Mystère du surnaturel* gets published no matter
what.[1] That book must not be allowed to get lost
in the shuffle.

Yes, H. M. L.'s (Ledesma's) letter made me
laugh, too. Enclosed please find a copy of my answer (you can return it at your convenience) that,
at my request, won't be published. Nevertheless
Van Ackeren has had it sent to H. M. L., with
apologies to me for having even thought of publishing the good Father's letter. It was ill-advised,
he told me, since H. M. L. was wrong. By the
way, Pegis is ready—yes, Pegis too—to put in his
two cents' worth. But this is just idle chatter.[2]

In a short time my *Metaphysics, Part I* will be printed. It's only a textbook, but I had to write it, if only to have something to go with *Natural Theology*. I'll see that Fourvière gets a copy.

These International Congresses—I'm too old to go to them any more. . . .

[1] I had developed, little by little, a study on *Le Mystère du surnaturel*, first published, after receiving special approval from Father-General John Janssens, in *Recherches de science religieuse* in 1949. I had just written to Father Smith about it; I had hardly thought of publishing it in its new form, fearing that it might be, as they say, warmed-over.

[2] Father Van Ackeren, S.J., director of the *Theology Digest* (with a large circulation in America), had reprinted in a 1960 issue, a series of valuable articles, one of which was by Father Smith, on the question of the supernatural. A really bad article, a diatribe full of errors, had somehow slipped into the series, and it gave quite a few theologians in the United States and Canada a terrific shock.

## 6

Marquette University
Milwaukee 3, Wisconsin

February 15, 1961

Dear Father Henri,

You told me your *Mystère du Surnaturel* will perhaps never be published.

Suppose *I* could find you a publisher here in the United States. Further, let's say I take charge of getting it translated into English, and having it approved by our ecclesiastical censors here. Then, would you still be determined not to do anything more with that book?

Pegis' letter, enclosed, will explain to you how and why I'm asking you these questions.[1]

Best wishes to you, in Our Lord,

G. SMITH, S.J.[2]

[1] Father Smith had consulted his (and Gilson's) friend, Anton G. Pegis, on this matter. Pegis was director of a collection of works being published by the Toronto Pontifical Institute, and he had given Father Smith an encouraging response on February 14.

[2] From Father Smith, on February 28, on receiving my answer to his proposal: "Overjoyed to get your 'maybe I'll have a go at it'. . . . I'll hang on until the temptation has taken hold of you to the point that you'll give in and do this for the cause of good. . . ."

## 7

Marquette University
Milwaukee 3, Wisconsin

July 19, 1965

Dear Father Henri, Christ's Peace!

Before I even begin to discuss your two wonderful
books[1] (that will come later), or about the Molina
business . . ., I'm hastening to invite you, in the
name of the University and of Father Bernard
Cooke, S.J., dean of the Faculty of Theology at
Marquette, to come to visit us after your stay at
Notre Dame. . . . No speeches, no hassles, no
ceremonies; quite simply a gathering of friends
who will find something to talk about with no
lectures necessary: *cor ad cor loquetur* [Heart will
speak to heart; tense change on Newman's famous
motto—Tr.].

Now to the Molina business,[2] it's amazing how
Providence has worked that out. Only three weeks
ago, Father G. Van Ackeren, S.J., professor in
the Scholasticate in St. Marys, Kansas, asked my
permission to publish this piece. "But, it was the

Censors at St. Marys who turned it down thirty years ago", I told him. "I know", he said, "but publishing it now would sort of make up for all that in one fell swoop." "Fine, go to it. Except, I won't revise it. I won't even correct the misprints, and you'll state all of that in print at the top of page one, adding that it was written thirty years ago." So, in spite of everything, perhaps my child "Molina and Liberty" will see the light of day.

At the moment, I'm in the process of preparing a few remarks on the subject of *Scholasticism in the Modern World* for the Convention of the American Catholic Philosophical Association in Washington in 1966. To sum it up, I'm going to comment on Gilson's text that you placed at the beginning of *Surnaturel*.[3] ("Buried under more than five centuries of deposits, ignorance of itself is the most serious ill from which Scholasticism is suffering. . . ."[4] Pegis will be there to point out the ills caused by this ignorance in the area of philosophy; I'll address theology: on the lack of appreciation of Holy Scripture, of the Church, of the person, of history, etc.) We absolutely have to eradicate these evils and be done with them. Right now it seems to me that the common and philosophical source of this ignorance, is not knowing the sense of eternal power in action, that is, God, and not understanding a being caused by God the way God understands that being; in other words, ignorance of Saint Thomas' metaphysics.

Best wishes to you in Our Lord,

GERRY SMITH

[1] *Augustinisme et théologie moderne* and *Le Mystère du surnaturel* (1965).

[2] See above, Smith's L. 1.

[3] Actually, at the beginning of *Le Mystère du surnaturel*. This book is dedicated to Father Smith, "as a mark of fraternal gratitude", since, having known for many years that this book existed in manuscript, and appreciating its contents, he wanted to publish it in America.

[4] The end of the citation: "To cure it, let us listen to the counsel of history: Return to theology" (É. Gilson, "Les recherches historico-critiques et l'avenir de la scolastique", in *Scholastica ratione historico-critica instauranda* [Rome, 1951], 142.

# APPENDIX IV

# AUTOGRAPH LETTER[1] FROM PAUL VI "TO THE ESTEEMED PROFESSOR É. GILSON, OUR SON IN JESUS CHRIST"

The Vatican
April 8, 1975

Notwithstanding your modesty, the passage of time has not eclipsed the merits you have earned, both by your intellectual activity over such a long period and of such vast extent, as well as by your exemplary fidelity to the Church. Giving thanks to Our Lord for the years you have filled with such good work, years that have made such an efficacious contribution to the spread of Christian thought, We have to express personally to you today an esteem We have long held for you, along with the gratitude you deserve from the Church.

Your teaching career in the French universities, notably at the Sorbonne and the Collège de France, or, in addition, at Harvard, then at Toronto, where you founded the Institute of Mediaeval Studies, not forgetting the lectures you have given at Our Lateran University; the *Archives d'histoire doctrinale et littéraire du Moyen Age*, founded and built up for many years under your conscientious guidance; finally and above all, the solid books you have published, place you in the first rank among those who have introduced Our contemporaries to the often forgotten or rejected riches of medieval philosophy. The Church, as an institution expert in humanity, can only rejoice in what you have accomplished.

Among the many representatives of this philosophy, your preferences straightaway turned toward Saint Thomas. You knew how to set forth the originality of Thomism by showing how the Angelic Doctor—enlightened by Christian revelation, in particular by the dogma of the creation and by what you call the "metaphysics of the Exodus"[2]—arrived at the inspired and truly novel notion of the "act of being", *ipsum esse*. From that point on, his philosophy stood on quite a different plane from Aristotle's. Thus, you have rekindled a source of wisdom from which our technically-oriented society should draw great profit, fascinated as it is by "having", but often blind to the sense of "being" and to its metaphysical roots.[3]

Moreover, your interest is not limited to Saint Thomas. Saint Augustine, Saint Bernard, Saint Bonaventure, Duns Scotus have all been subjects of your studies. In these works, as in those of a more general nature on "philosophy in the Middle Ages" and on the "spirit of medieval philosophy", a great idea stands out that is particularly dear to Us: the Faith is not something to hinder or extinguish thought or human culture, but a light and a stimulant. It is within the context of theology, in the light of Revelation, that philosophical thought, notably in Saint Thomas' case, has reached its summits. How We would wish that the younger generations, worn down by atheist ideologies, might rediscover in this School the productivity of the Faith, at the same time as they regain confidence in reason as one of the Creator's gifts!

Besides, your work, so rich and so varied, which has long made you worthy of the honor of a seat in the Académie française, of becoming a member of the Roman Academy of Saint Thomas Aquinas and the Catholic Religion, and of receiving so many academic distinctions, well demonstrates how the Faith welcomes and favors the most authentic humanism. Your attention as a philosopher and as a historian has fallen upon the most diverse disciplines, whenever they touched on the functions of mankind and of civilization: literature—how could one not call to mind here your studies on Dante—art, language, biology, social culture, have all brought forth your comments and publications. Like your friend

Maritain, you have known how to make today's Christians, and many other men of good will, so often troubled and alienated, appreciate words of good sense, words of wisdom, words of faithfulness.

Above all, dear Professor—this is one of the points that impresses Us most at this present time—you have spent your efforts and shown your Christian Faith in the bosom of the Catholic Church, whom you have always regarded as a mother. You have received from her, with confidence, all that she could offer you concerning the mysteries of God. You have labored loyally for her, rendering her one of the most distinguished contributions in philosophy to fulfill the needs of her pastoral apostolate. You have borne witness in her favor. You have suffered, and you suffer with her, because of those things that would mar her beauty. You have unfailingly given her your trust and your affection.[4]

May the Lord cause what you have sown with so much patience to grow! May he make your witness fruitful! May he raise up more strong advocates of Christian philosophy! And may he fill *you* with his peace! As for Us, with all Our heart, in token of these blessings and in witness to Our constant esteem, We extend to you Our affectionate Apostolic Benediction.

PAULUS PP. VI

[1] This letter was published in *L'Osservatore romano*, September 11, 1975, and reprinted in *Documentation catholique*, vol. 72 (October 5, 1975): col. 812–813.

[2] "In the autograph letter Paul VI sent to Étienne Gilson on April 8, 1975, the day after his ninetieth birthday, the Pope told him: 'You knew how to set forth the originality of Thomism', and he said this, calling special attention to 'what you [Gilson] call the *metaphysics* of the Exodus'. This expression apparently does not mean that the Angelic Doctor and his interpreter took the book of Exodus to be a treatise on metaphysics, but they uncovered the metaphysical truth implicit in the scene lit by the flames of a 'bush that was all on fire' and yet 'was not consumed': there, Moses asks God to tell him his name and God answers: 'I AM that I AM.' The translation is of little importance; it matters more what the answer, so translated, became, in the thirteenth century, in the new philosophy: Plato's Good and Plotinus' One are, in a way, absorbed into Being with a capital letter on whom all beings without capital letters depend, the principle *and end* of everything that exists. In Saint Thomas' thought, then in Gilson's, this is the center where everything begins and where everything ends.

"And Gilson wrote copiously to defend and to illustrate this inexhaustible truth. Even after the new edition, revised and augmented, of his great work *L'Être et l'Essence*, in 1962, he still had the feeling there was something more to be said: the partially unedited volume he left behind bears this meaningful title: *Constants philosophiques de l'Être . . .*" (H. Gouhier, speech on his reception into the Académie française [1979], in *Étienne Gilson et nous*, 155).

[3] "By reading and rereading Saint Thomas with a humble spirit and an open mind, states that merely indicate the desire to learn, one is often struck by the particular strength or clarity of certain formulae. I have often noticed several of them, especially those that shed some light on certain aspects

of the notion of being (*esse*) as Saint Thomas conceived it. As soon as I thought I understood it, it became the heart of his doctrine as far as I was concerned. It seems to me that it provides the way to go as far as one can toward the source of the great metaphysical renewal Saint Thomas accomplished. All I wanted to do in those few preceding pages was to leave behind me a witness to this way of understanding Thomistic doctrine. I would almost have given in to the temptation to call these notes: "My Saint Thomas Aquinas", if I had been sure of making it understood that all I meant by that was what had nourished my metaphysical ideas throughout the years, in the Master's doctrine. Fascinated since early youth by the notion of being and its primordial importance, I could never detach myself from Saint Thomas, beginning with the day I understood that for him too, everything began with his notion, if it is a notion, and everything had to come back to it . . ." (É. Gilson, "Éléments d'une métaphysique thomiste de l'être", in *Archives d'histoire doctrinale et littéraire du Moyen Age*, année 1973 [Vrin, 1974]: 7–36 [p. 35]).

[4] This testimony of approval was perfectly designed to console Gilson for the lack of understanding (that sometimes extended to verbal abuse) from which he suffered throughout the last ten years of his life, from the many "postconciliar" innovators. But in France, the Pope's words hardly had even a faint echo.

# APPENDIX V

# É. GILSON, FATHER BALIĆ, AND THE SCHOLASTIC FAMILIES

In September 1950—just before the third International Thomist Congress held under the auspices of the Pontifical Academy of Saint Thomas Aquinas—there took place in Rome an "International Scholastic Congress". The idea for it was suggested by Father Charles Balić, a Franciscan, the magnificent rector of the Antonianum. Its goal was not only to encourage scholarly studies of the ancient Scholastic doctrines: it was especially to show the value of these doctrines' vitality, still viable to this very day, in all their pluralism. More precisely, Father Balić wanted to illustrate by means of this Congress that Thomism was not the Church's only method of presenting theology and the "Christian philosophy" recommended by the popes with an insistence that had accrued since the encyclical *Aeterni patris* of Leo XIII. Hence the name "Congress on Modern Scholasticism" applied by some to the project.

Balić was "Gilson's good friend"; he thought highly of Gilson's integrity and the strength of his work; he considered him a "great scholar". Gilson gladly accepted the invitation to speak at the Congress. He took as the subject of his talk: "Duns Scotus in the light of historical criticism. Historico-critical research and the future of Scholasticism. The Prologues of the *Opus oxoniensis*" (*Acta* [Rome, 1951]; English résumé in *The Modern Schoolman* [1951]: "Historical research and the future of Scholasticism"). This was to fulfill Father Balić's wish—but in his own way, by presenting for the first time in public, in all its forcefulness and paradoxical clarity, the twofold thesis that had been imposing itself more and more on his mind: on the theological origin and foundation of medieval philosophy and on its permanent role as "handmaid" of theology, a role to which philosophy must remain faithful to have any future at all. He was not unhappy to have this opportunity offered him as an occasion on which to drop his "bombshell", that, in the event, went off just as he had planned, producing a stunned reaction in his hearers.

Even Phelan, when he read the summary of the lecture in *The Modern Schoolman* shortly afterward, was disconcerted. He wrote to a friend that "for the first time" in his life he no longer agreed with Gilson, and he could no longer tell his students: "Read Gilson!" It was hardly more than a provisional misunderstanding between the two men, at least as far as the first part of the thesis was concerned: Gilson did not, as Phelan had first thought, want to exclude the study of classical philosophers, nor to belittle the medieval thinkers' obvious debt to them; for his own part, Phelan preferred to call the Church Fathers "Commentators of the Church" and not "theologians". . . .[1]

By his resounding intervention at the "Scholastic Congress", Gilson undoubtedly wanted to define his personal position versus all the modern factions within the group, the most powerful of whom were to hold court starting the following day; and already his very presence at this first Congress clearly showed his independence from the "Thomist" clique that currently advertised itself as the exclusive organ of Catholic orthodoxy.

Early on, he became interested in Saint Francis and Franciscan thought. Between 1924 and 1931, he had collaborated very actively on the *Revue d'histoire franciscaine*, etc. His great work on the philosophy of Saint Bonaventure dated from 1924, and the one on John Duns Scotus, in preparation since 1924 in a series of courses, seminars, and many publications, came out in its finished form in 1952. Between 1951 and 1953, he had contributed three articles to the official journal *Antonianum*, etc. At the end of 1959, he received a visit from Balić in Paris. Balić, who had been working wholeheartedly for a long time in behalf of Duns

Scotus' canonization, had come to try to gain Gilson's support for his cause. Gilson was not at all against it. He had already received an inquiry in that regard from the competent Roman Congregation, and had written to Pegis about it: "Personally, I am in total disagreement with Duns Scotus; his is a climate of thought in which I can't survive; but I can't see that there's anything against him as far as his faith or his conduct are concerned"; he was only sorry that in their debates the Scotists were not "any more honorable than the Thomists".[2] This is just about what he must have told Balić, with a bit more subtlety: Duns Scotus was worthy of sainthood, Gilson had been praying for it for a long time, but he wished they would not try to canonize his doctrine along with him. . . .

This cool and conditional approval did no harm to their good relationship. Thus Balić, still hoping, invited Gilson again, several years later, to yet another Scotist Congress that was to be held in Rome in 1966. But this time Gilson asked to be excused, saying he had family problems. His true motive was otherwise. Already in 1950 he had not been pleased when he saw the "Scholastic Congress" turn into a Scotist Congress before his very eyes. Now things had become really serious. The Scotists no longer needed anyone to defend them, and he had no desire to be listed on their rolls. He explained himself openly in a letter he sent on October 3, 1966, to Father Maurer: "I used up all my ammunition in favor of Duns Scotus. Now that Scotism in Purgatory has become Scotism Triumphant, I've no further interest in it. I need Scotists in order to be free inside the Church. I've been disgusted with the slanders directed at Duns Scotus and the Scotists. Now that's all over and done with. Now Scotism is simply a doctrinal position opposed to Saint Thomas' true metaphysic of being. If I must choose between the *ens* without *esse* and the *ens habens esse*, I pick the latter. I now see coming the age of a Duns Scotus who is philosophically and theologically an anti-Thomas: in this eventuality, let me just abstain. They can take that as yet another example of 'late Gilsonism'. . . . But freedom, for me, isn't freedom to waffle: I am against the metaphysic of universal being."[3]

The abandonment of Saint Thomas by many of the clergy, during this time of uncontrolled volatility, was painful to Gilson, and maybe he was allowing himself to diagnose, in the ontology of the "anti-Thomas", the as yet deeply-buried root of modern apostasy. As for his talk of Scotism Triumphant . . . The whole of Scholasticism, from the best to the worst of it, seemed on a headlong downhill course toward self-destruction.[4] Let us remember, rather, to the everlasting credit of this great Thomist, that if he rejected any *system* that in its turn rejected another, he never tried to force us to choose between two irreconcilable *syntheses* born of the same faith. In his seminal work on *La Philosophie de saint Bonaventure*, he had written: "After Saint Bonaventure the mystical synthesis of medieval Augustinianism would no longer be necessary, just as after Saint Thomas the work of Christian Aristotelianism had nothing left to achieve"; their two philosophies "complement each other as the two most universal systems within Christianity, and it is because they are complementary that they can neither be mutually exclusive nor coincide". A generous and completely fair appraisal that does not try to slam the brakes on history, but offers us a twofold model, guiding without fixing the course of subsequent inquiry, always unpredictable, that every new age imposes on philosophy—as Gilson, always aware of history, observed more than once. In the dwelling-place of God, that is beyond all time, Bonaventure and Thomas are food and light, respectively, for our pilgrimage . . . "*Duae olivae et duo candelabra in domo Dei lucentia*".[5]

As Father Jacques-Guy Bourgerol noted, it must have taken some courage for this young university professor to undertake, right after the First World War, to "reestablish the precise truth about Saint Bonaventure".[6] But he wouldn't have needed courage to remain faithful to him, so happy was he to uncover that truth and subsequently to return to it again and again. And surely he must have closely observed that by very divergent paths, and each in his own way, Bonaventure and Thomas would meet each other on that great matter of our final end about which Gilson spoke to me in many of his letters.

He was less welcoming to Duns Scotus. He seems never to have seriously asked himself, throughout all his lengthy and decidedly perceptive analyses, whether it might not also be possible to distill from the historical Duns Scotus an eternal Scotism, capable of nourishing, for example, the reflections of a [Gerard Manley] Hopkins, as profound a thinker as he was a great poet, or of awakening the vocation to philosophy in a Fernand Guimet, dead before his time, who, while discharging the successive responsibilities of diocesan administrator, almoner for Secondary Education, and ecclesiastical counselor to our embassy to the Vatican, shunning all the narrowness and intrigue of the Schools, was working hard to finish a study on the Seraphic Doctor that would have been worthy of being appended to an edition of Gilson's own writings.

[1] Shook, *Gilson*, 296–300.
[2] February 25, 1950 (ibid., 297).
[3] In ibid., 373 (French translation). "Late Gilsonism": with a pejorative tinge, as one says "Late Empire". Cf. *Les Tribulations de Sophie*, 41–42.

[4] *La Philosophie de saint Bonaventure*, 3rd ed. (1953), 393–396. Note, however, with Jean-Robert Armogathe, that "the relationships between Étienne Gilson the philosopher and Étienne Gilson the historian have always been difficult" (in *Les Quatre fleuves* 10 [1979]).

[5] In *Étienne Gilson et nous*, 38.

[6] Cf. Hans Urs von Balthasar, *La Gloire et la Croix* 2:237–323: "Bonaventure", Théologie series, 74 [Aubier, 1968]).

# APPENDIX VI

# "THE BIG FAMILY OF 'THOMISTS'"

The expression is Gilson's own. (Note that he places the last word in quotation marks.) "It's rather a motley crew, but one gets used to it, although once crowned with this title, it may take one a while to adjust to wearing it."[1]

He himself did not join the "big family" right away. He took great care, for some time, to keep his distance. On the advice of his mentor Lévy-Bruhl, he approached "Scholasticism", a vast *terra incognita*, tentatively at first and purely as a historian, in order to understand Descartes better. His first course, at the University of Lille, on "Saint Thomas' system" may well have been seen as something of a revolution within the academic conception of the history of philosophy: he introduced a renewed curiosity to compensate for the long excommunication scornfulness had imposed. But he still lacked dedication. When Gilson gave six lectures at the University of Brussels on "Descartes and Scholastic metaphysics", in December

1923, ten years after his Sorbonne thesis, he still kept to the same strictly historical perspective. During this time he apparently took no part whatever in the publications and celebrations that accompanied Pius XI's encyclical *Studiorum ducem*. Even as late as 1925, it would be wrong to assume that he had become a Thomist. In no way whatsoever did he present himself as an apostle or defender of the Angelic Doctor. If he continued to study him, he also stood apart from the intellectual movement one of whose results was the creation of the *Bulletin thomiste*, the organ of the "Thomist Society". Only later did he collaborate on the *Revue de philosophie*, published by the Institut catholique de Paris. "It is significant", Father Shook observes (p. 116), "that, when the *Bulletin thomiste* took note of his works and those of his students Gouhier and Koyré, the catalogue was entitled: 'Le thomisme et les non-scolastiques'. This distinction must have pleased Gilson."

However, such a situation (or such discretion) could not last long. In that same year 1925, Jacques Maritain, who did not yet know the distinguished "professor of the history of medieval philosophies" (or had only just met him), and who had embraced, in a "second conversion", the brand of Thomism espoused by his revered spiritual director Father Clérissac, O.P., in a purely doctrinal way, already suspected that Gilson's "strictly historical" position was also "strictly provisional". The truth is that for no more reason than his work's success, the brilliant historian was soon to become one of the great *leaders* of the Thomist movement. He would become more and more influential.[2] A passionate interest, a fervent loyalty, would take the place of wise reserve under a thin veneer of indifference, and would cause him to become a member of the "big family"—albeit always "without swearing fealty to it". So it was that he was going to be thrust into multiple battles in a lengthy social conflict. By taking on the whole family, he constantly found himself at odds with one or another of its numerous branches—and the feuding, that he did not seem to consider totally distasteful, was sometimes savage.

The Suarezians were excommunicated in advance. All those who called themselves pure Thomists supported Gilson in that. Yet, at least as second-cousins, the Suarezians made up a large part of the family. When they proclaimed themselves "authorized" interpreters of the Universal Doctor, they were within their rights, and not just because of privileges granted them undeservedly: after all, even in the cadre of the purest "Thomists", were there not many who had put forward fundamental theses that Suarez had picked up from the "great commentators"?[3] And did the Suarezian Descoqs not go out of his way to affect admiration for Cajetan, the Thomist authority par excellence? To bid higher, if one has to admit that the *"aggiornamento"*, as Gilson calls it, "of the Thomist metaphysic" undertaken by Suarez was hardly authentic, would there not also be reasons to suggest that "the admirable structure of Wolff's ontology", as Gilson also says with tongue in cheek, might update it even more? Yet this too has left no less a mark on some of the most intransigent Thomists, indeed the most official[4] ones, even if they have never read Wolff.

There was, in the first third of this century, a hybrid created by crossing Thomism with the "Action française" movement that could count some great names among its adherents; it attracted many intellectuals, and infiltrated even into the pockets of "conservatism". Léon Daudet's sonorous voice recruited its neophytes from his vast public. The more somber tones of Charles Maurras sang a hymn to the "white light" that, thanks to the great Cardinal Mercier, cast a different glow over Saint Thomas and his teacher from Stagira [i.e., Aristotle—Tr.], revealing to us the secret of all things, teaching us a different lesson about the ruling hierarchies, calling our attention to truths that would allow us to win through to the heart of reality. . . .[5] This kind of Thomism, that created rumblings within the Church, evidently could not find favor with our solid doctrinal historian, no less a solid republican in his politics. Finally, after having openly demanded an autocracy of intelligence coupled with orthodoxy, it understandably was bound to collapse.

More worrisome was the low-profile work coming from an erudite school whose most famous member, at least in France, was Father Mandonnet, O.P. From their research an entirely new Saint Thomas surged forth. But there was something disturbing about his titanic form. If he succeeded in slicing Averroës or Siger de Brabant in two with one blow of his terrible, swift sword, his Aristotelian complexion only gave him reason to cast slurs that almost amounted to violence on any kind of Augustinianism. On the heels of this modern, educated restoration, the recently-invented hydra of "political Augustinianism" presented itself as a likely victim to more than one Thomist; the monster finally received its mortal wound from none other than Thomas Aquinas, the Archangel Gabriel of secularism.[6] Now, in Gilson's eyes, secularism was a new idol he proposed to smash on its own territory—history—by putting forward a better analysis. The campaign, conducted unemotionally, was to be a long one. "Réflexions sur la controverse saint Thomas–saint Augustin", published in 1930 in the first volume of *Mélanges Mandonnet*, was only one of the first episodes, and the fresh explanations added in 1943, with the new editions of *Saint Thomas* and *Saint Bonaventure*, did not even come close to bringing things to an end.[7]

While Gilson admired Rousselot, immediately singling him out as bearing the mark of genius, he hardly had time for a more recent work, akin to Rousselot's and springing from a similar bent: Joseph Maréchal, S.J., was trying to provide a new access to Thomist metaphysics by comparing it with Kant's great philosophical system, using a critical approach that tried to assimilate the two sets of ideas. Such an undertaking, for all its boldness, austerity, and rigor, was too foreign to Gilson's own orientation to escape his criticism, but it evidently didn't hold his attention for very long.[8]

The neo-Thomist group from the University of Louvain[9] was Gilson's principal opponent in the bosom of the "big family", the clique with whom he was to remain in drawn-out, nearly permanent, conflict. He had two bones to pick with these disciples of Cardinal Mercier (1851–1926): first, that they had cobbled up a Thomsitic philosophy so independent of Christian theology as to be absolutely separate from it,[10] and second, that they had consequently tried to use this philosophy to confront present-day problems, while paying no attention to Saint Thomas. Such an effort seemed sterile to Gilson. In his view, to extract a pure philosophy from the Thomist synthesis in order to turn its author into the "apostle of modern times", was to harm him and themselves at once. In short, he rejected out of hand the distortion of the real Saint Thomas together with the utopianism of trying to do such a thing in the first place.

At the root of this philosophical debate lay a problem in methodology. The men from Louvain based their work on Mercier's *Critérologie générale* and Noël's *Notes d'épistémologie thomiste*. Gilson had criticized these works in a series of articles he collected into one volume in 1935: *Le Réalisme méthodique*, the opposite of their "critical realism". For their part, the Louvain team, caught off guard when this newcomer broke in on the scene, little grasping Saint Augustine's hold—as both a brother-in-arms and at the same time a bosom enemy—over this odd Thomist Gilson, could not hide the fact that Gilson made them a bit nervous.

It was a long, more or less amicable joust. At the smallest opportunity, the offensive would pass from one side to the other, and the counter-attack came without delay. Gilson manifested his disagreement as soon as Monsignor Simon Deploige put out, in its third edition, *Le Conflit de la morale et de la sociologie*, despite Maritain's approval in a preface welcoming the work into its series.[11] When Gilson himself explained his conclusions on liberty and theology according to Descartes to the French Philosophical Society, he found himself eyeball to eyeball with Maurice de Wulf, the prize-winning historian of medieval philosophy, who had come to object: What is theology doing here? Another time (it was in 1936), Gilson dug up this assertion in a work inspired by Mercier: "God's existence cannot be the object of an act of faith in God", and he did not miss the opportunity to declare that untenable;[12] but Monsignor Noël, in defense of the head of his school, wriggled out of the discussion by claiming that those words had been interpolated by an over-enthusiastic disciple. . . .[13] Joining with Mandonnet, the scholars from Louvain protested against the title of philosopher that Gilson had lavished upon Saint Augustine: Gilson stuck to his guns—without ever succeeding in getting them to concede, in any sense that they could accept, his concept of "Christian philosophy", a tag just as dear to him. His toughest adversary—but at the same time a loyal friend—was Canon Fernand Van Steenberghen: this man wrote against him in the *Revue néoscolastique*, sent him letters on top of letters, pursued him even into his country place, was ready to contradict him every time they attended conventions together. They both thought highly of each other, but on the most crucial point, not even the least bit of agreement between the two was possible. Neither Van Steenberghen nor his colleagues could understand that "a Catholic's only chance to become a great philosopher is to be basically a theologian".[14] Gilson was, to them, a paradox that would always require them to square the circle. And the result of their incessant critiques was that, by forcing the master from Paris and Toronto to explain himself better and better, they anchored him more and more firmly in the positions that would be the ones he took in his last writings.[15]

. . . So, here we are in Rome, in 1950, where the Louvain team, clashing with the same enemy that this Thomist without a membership card knew how to scrap with so well, suddenly find themselves on Gilson's side, to the last man. Of course, he still insists that he does not want a formal distinction to be taken to mean a separation, and his "Christian philosophy" still seems to them to muddle everything up—but he knows as well as they do how to make a distinction when he has to, using whatever arguments fit the bill, between an academic discussion and a private opinion imposed with the force of an edict. The important thing, for now, is: there is nothing more comforting than putting up a common defense against the attack of a common enemy. And he will receive his reward without undue delay: for the inauguration of the "Cardinal Mercier Chair" of philosophy, that took place on April 23, 1952, Étienne Gilson was invited to Louvain,[16] and he gave ten lectures there, from which developed his book on *Les Métamorphoses de la Cité de Dieu*.[17]

Within the "big Thomist family" of the twentieth century, Maritain occupies a place of importance. There, he plays a role that attracts and repels at the same time. At the already rather late date of September 1930, he got to know Gilson, as a result of being introduced through the efforts of Charles Du Bos. They met many times. Gilson had Maritain come to the Toronto Pontifical Institute; in 1945 he announced Maritain's appointment as ambassador to the Vatican in *La Vie intellectuelle*; he helped him to win the grand prize of the Académie française. A common admiration for Saint Thomas' genius brought the two men together, the realism they shared caused them to react about the same way (although their reactions took different forms) to teachers of philosophy whom Maritain named the "idéosophes" [philosophers of self—Tr.]. Both men suffered, in the twilight of their lives, from having to see the Thomists deny publicly the very things that had formed both of their philosophical personalities; they judged with the same amount of severity, if not according to the same methods of diagnosis, the "self-destruction of the Church" Paul VI had denounced. However, as much as they both would have preferred to avoid confrontations with one another, they followed different roads from personal preference as often as their strong personalities would have forced them to take opposite directions anyway. According to Shook, who had a great deal of inside information, if they remained good friends, they were nevertheless "in acute disagreement on quite a few essential points".[18]

Thomistically, Maritain admitted Gilson to his inner circle, in the company of "Garrigou-Lagrange, Tonquédec, Peillaube, Cordovani. . . ." The differences which had always existed among them all were, according to Maritain, "of the order of those divergences that, developing over a fundamental agreement in philosophy, give promise of a cooperative venture that could make real progress on philosophical questions".[19] But this was drafting Gilson rather precipitately . . . Gilson's choices for this circle, or his ideas on who should be excluded, were still not the same as Maritain's, far from it. Would Maritain have gladly made room for Sertillanges in his closed corporation?[20] Would he have seen Rousselot as the "primary spokesman for this revival of Saint Thomas' Thomism, that would free us from so many uncertainties"?[21] Would he have been ready to work together with someone like Gabriel Marcel, in whom Gilson recognized not only perhaps the most authentic and most profound philosopher of our time, but a true heir of the metaphysic of Being?[22]

It is known that Gilson, like many others, was shocked by Maritain's book on Bergson. As late as 1959, in a letter to Pegis, after mentioning how much he had liked Maritain, he added: "However, there's one thing I can't forgive him for, his book on Bergson. . . . There wouldn't have been any problem if only he hadn't brandished Thomism like a club. . . ." The fact is that even Maritain's warmest admirers, such as the Rev. Henry Bars,[23] cannot find any excuse for this book except to suggest that at the time the young philosopher was under a lot of pressure.[24] But Gilson's distress goes beyond the level of personalities; he reveals a grave dissatisfaction with his intellectual attitude: "I get something out of Maritain," he says to Pegis, "just as I get something out of Bergson, and as I'm sure I'd get something out of Heidegger if I could understand him better. I'm not worried about how far Maritain agrees with Saint Thomas. It's just that when I see him jump on Bergson in Saint Thomas' name, and maybe at the same time poorly understanding Thomas himself, I can't keep from saying something. . . ."[25]

Did both men see Saint Thomas in precisely the same way? On the one hand, it was a matter of a Saint Thomas whose text was certainly not rejected, but, all too often, was read through the spectacles of the "great commentators" (a sacrosanct label: those who snapped their fingers at it were made laughing-stocks). Their interpretation had the force of law; according to them was understood and regulated "the theological doctrine that distinguished the natural order from the super-natural order, an inflexible distinction dearer to the Catholic Faith than the apple of an eye, as important and vital for the town as for the Church, for a sound understanding of nature as for matters having to do with grace, and whose entire ratio-nale was developed over the course of centuries, in a long, sometimes rather accidental *fieri*, before reaching its full maturity. . . ."[26] No Catholic could refuse to accept the "theological doctrine", recalled by the commentators "in principle", nec-essary to the "Catholic Faith". But Gilson, a wiser man because he was a historian, and therefore a better Thomist, was at liberty to understand these principles in the same way Saint Thomas himself did; whereas Maritain was always looking at them in a sense put forward later, in a drastically mod-ified philosophical context, by men like Cajetan or John of Saint Thomas.[27] Their Faith was the same, it was as dear to one as it was to the other, but they differed radically as to which was the right philosophico-theological synthesis to ex-press that Faith's "entire rationale" and as to the century when the rationale came to maturity (only Gilson had a clear understanding of this question of date). Their divergence was obvious. When he was invited to Princeton in 1953, Gilson seems to have on that occasion either planted or at least encouraged a doubt in Maritain's mind about the Thomist exegeses for which the two "great commentators" were responsible. Maritain said later, as if he had lost interest, that "Gilson no doubt was right", but without appearing to notice that his own synthesis, in whose name he had judged Thomist—and even Catholic—orthodoxy, would be turned upside down if this were so. He was to abandon, "not without regret", Cajetan, "that incomparable reasoner, Aristotle's sectary, alas, in a way that Saint Thomas was not", but he pled for John of Saint Thomas: "The Commentator I love—whom I'm not afraid to differ from if I have to[28]—is not Cajetan, it's John of Saint Thomas, who, in spite of his interminable sentences and his charming intoxication with the technicalities of logic, was basically a man of *intuition*."[29] This, however, is the same fundamental error in interpretation that Gilson had denounced in both commentators. But Maritain's ingenuous eclecticism, that forced him to choose between the two hoary commentators who, to Gilson's mind, could not be separated, at the same time made him lump together as the two best current interpreters of the Angel of the School, Étienne Gilson, the author of *L'esprit de la philosophie médiévale*, and Father Garrigou-Lagrange, the author of *La Philosophie de l'être et le sens commun*.[30]

A further difference between our two Thomist friends. For Maritain, Saint Thomas is a true philosopher, while with Saint Augustine, despite his gift of wisdom, philosophy has "not yet found its footing";[31] his doctrine is not a metaphysic in the proper sense of the word; it is an "infused" wisdom, a "wisdom of grace", whereas Saint Thomas' is "theological wisdom": "Thomism is the scientific state of Christian wisdom." By these distinctions, Maritain does not mean to denigrate Saint Augustine's work, nor to take issue with Saint Thomas' "absolutely perfect fidelity to Saint Augustine in his theological synthesis"; but Saint Thomas has, besides, "metaphysical wisdom", of which one finds in Saint Augustine only the first "stammerings". Augustine's "ways of approach . . . consisted more in a loving meditation on the things of God than in the search for an explanation strictly grounded in reason." And then Maritain cited Gilson's words: "One could say that the substance of Augustinianism passed whole and entire into the *Summa Theologiae*"; but with this immediate proviso: "With plenty of revisions, it goes without saying," in trying "to make clear, to save, the truth of this or that thesis whose formula was inadmissible. To save all the truths that had ever been spoken (and often ill-spoken) in his presence, *there* was the task assigned to Saint Thomas".[32] And Gilson led him back, answering with a twinkle, as if to reiterate the appropriateness of his term: "Whatever you may say, Augustine was not completely unworthy of the title, philosopher."[33] Further, Maritain knew very well that Saint Thomas wrote the *Summa Theologiae* that he himself respected and put into practice, that he even hymns with a sometimes disproportionate lyricism:[34] nevertheless, he was "more and more persuaded that his philosophy, . . . kept under wraps for centuries, enveloped in theological terminology", must finally "take its proper shape . . . and its independent development": he wanted it "separated for its own sake" and "returned to its proper nature as philosophy": which would be, as he was fond of saying, the "philosophy of Aristotle and of Saint Thomas", "entirely transfigured", as he defined it, in its metaphysical aspect by the "extraordinary philosophical genius" of Saint Thomas.[35] Gilson's approach was not exactly contradictory, but the other way around. In his view, "you change Saint Thomas' theological thought if you imagine that it could be tied in with any philosophical doctrine whatsoever, even one that a theologian would judge from a distance to be the best of all"; likewise the other way around, and more and more insistent, was the watchword he gave to the Thomists of our own day, which he repeated in the slogan: "Put theology first."[36]

It is well known that for Maritain, Saint Thomas is the "apostle of modern times". This characterization, that had been disputed by Henri Gouhier,[37] was to be taken up again and commented upon at length in 1930 in *Le Docteur angélique*. Gilson, who agreed with Gouhier (because "to be the apostle of modern times presupposes that the apostle will answer the questions modern times ask"), warns today's Thomist to be even more on guard, lest he think he is capable of solving, in Saint Thomas' name, the new problems the new schools pose, notably those of the different forms of existentialism: this brand of Thomist would be an "unacceptable apologist". Nor would he have voluntarily agreed with Maritain, who said that "Thomist philosophy is in itself a missionary philosophy".[38] The same generalized difference in the two men's orientation also appears to explain why Gilson stuck with "methodological realism", refusing to poke his finger into the fatal mechanism of criteriologies, while Maritain, who like Gilson eschewed as illusory "the efforts of many contemporary neo-Scholastics to bring realism in through the doors Descartes and Kant opened for idealism", thought, no less than the scholars of Louvain did, that today it is necessary to use "critical realism"[39] to correct "spontaneous realism".

In the passage from *Réflexions sur l'intelligence* cited above (cf. note 21), after concluding that the Catholic doctrine of the supernatural finds its correct expression and "its point of completion in Saint Thomas' thought", Maritain made this remark: "Hence it follows that quite a few rough guesses were permitted before Saint Thomas, that one cannot get away with any more." He was trying to be indulgent toward Saint Augustine (who after all was privileged to represent only the first twelve centuries of Christian thought), but at the same time he was damning everybody who, since the death of Saint Thomas, had had the bad luck to miss this "point of completion", be it by ever so little. But since, whenever Maritain says "Saint Thomas", Gilson obliges us to read in "Cajetan" and all of his ilk, Saint Thomas himself, who preceded them, escaped condemnation only thanks to Maritain's generosity toward Augustine and the whole varicolored throng that went before him. To my mind, this is the main philosophico-theological breach between Maritain's and Gilson's respective Thomisms. Seen from this angle, the Thomism of Maritain (whom Gilson, in an appreciation shot through with humor, presented as a "paléo-thomiste"[40]), looks like another form of neo-Thomism among all the others, albeit a particularly important one.

Both Gilson and Maritain took a constant interest in the problem of the nature of art. About 1915, when Gilson was at the Verdun front, he wrote up his ideas on "Art et métaphysique", publishing them in the *Revue de métaphysique et de morale* in 1916; they provided the basis for an *Introduction aux arts du beau* that came out a half-century later (1963). In 1920, Maritain produced a pamphlet, *Art et scolastique*, that he enlarged in subsequent editions of *Frontières de la poésie* and in several appendices. On the relationships between art and moral philosophy, these two Christian philosophers could not help being in basic agreement. In the chapter on "L'artiste et le saint" that concludes *L'école des muses*, Gilson constructed a fine parallel whose magnificent lines converge with Maritain's. The few differences between the two men resulted from the fact that Maritain worked with poetry uppermost in his mind, while Gilson's interests led him more toward painting: hence, Gilson's unwillingness to entertain the expression "creative intuition" that Maritain wanted to use as a definition of art. Yet, there was a still deeper gulf that separated them. Maritain, faithful to the method inculcated on him when he first became a Thomist, still sought doctrinal bases in the "great commentators". (In the second edition of *Art et scolastique*, Cajetan is cited seven times, John of Saint Thomas eleven.) From John of Saint Thomas, Maritain borrowed a few words of Aristotle's that had filtered down through Saint Thomas, with which to concoct, after the manner of this favorite commentator, a definition of art. Gilson thought this was the wrong way to go about it. Saint Thomas, he felt, probably did not have "much of a taste for the fine arts" and seems never to have thought deeply about them; therefore, to work up from one or two words of his a theory to answer our modern questions, would this not amount to jumping with all four feet into the sort of neo-Thomism whose counter-productivity needed no further demonstration?[41]

Gilson was not unaware of the "very original" quality of the notions set forth in *Art et scolastique*, meditation on which, he admitted, could be useful—but he still felt estranged. Not entertaining the "least unfriendly sentiment" toward the author, he did not want to get into an argument with him. However, about 1955, the head-on collision that had been waiting to happen supervened. Gilson, needing to crystallize his own position, decided that it was at last time to compare his ideas with Maritain's. *Painting and Reality* was published in New York in 1957.[42] "The result was", he wrote later to his friend Pegis, "that I was run out of the Garden of Eden by an angry angel, whose job it was to defend the truth about poetry with a flaming sword." The furious angel, as Shook explains for us, turned out to be Raïssa. As Gilson had suspected from the beginning, and as many successive dedications of *Art et scolastique* revealed for all to see, she was "primarily responsible for whatever Maritain had written on the subject"; in addition to taking an active part in the editing, she was the one who "had goaded her husband toward a theory of aesthetics that had little to do with Saint Thomas".[43]

It did not, however, prove to be an irremediable quarrel: the *Mélanges Gilson*, published the following year, contained a fine study by Maritain on

"Socrate et la philosophie morale" (note, however, that the subject he chose allowed him to avoid any mention of art or of Saint Thomas). But the sense of incompatibility persisted, as again was evident in the new book Gilson published in 1964, on *Matières et formes*.[44]

⚜

"The art of being a Thomist" is a difficult one. . . . In the "big family" of Thomists, each one understands that art and devotes himself to practicing it in his own way. An "apprenticeship" is required, and it is not the same for everybody. Thus, in an effort to be wise as well as charitable, the Thomist Gilson proposed that anyone who calls himself a disciple, when speaking for himself alone, ought simply to recount his personal experience and leave everyone else out of it.[45]

Monsignor Fernand Guimet, a fervent Scotist who knew this century's theological history inside and out, spoke one day to the CCIF (Centre Catholique des Intellectuels Français) about "this protean neo-Thomism that, for a little less than a century, has sheltered the most varied, indeed sometimes the most questionable, projects under its noble umbrella".[46] It would be hard not to agree with him. I have chosen not to go into details. Saint Thomas' reputation has suffered from these distortions, to the great detriment of our generation. One may hope, at least, that those who take up Scholasticism in the future will not, once again, fall into the same traps.

[1] *Philosophe et théologie,* 216.

[2] In a note to Raïssa's *Journal,* relating to a fragment of a letter that seems to date from 1931, Jacques Maritain says that Charles Du Bos, Mauriac, Gabriel Marcel, and even Gilson were at that time "opposed to the philosophical approach that Raïssa and I considered then, and have always considered, the only true one". But, he continues, "soon the progress of Gilson's thought would bring him to admit the primacy of Saint Thomas Aquinas over all the other masters, however great, of the Middle Ages, and to start his own thinking along the ways Saint Thomas had opened" (p. 206).

[3] "Suarez is halfway between Saint Thomas' metaphysics and the eighteenth-century metaphysics of Wolff . . .": É. Gilson, *Constantes métaphysiques de l'être,* 69. (On the subject of Suarez, see von Balthasar, *Gloire et Croix* 2:96–102, under the title: "L'être comme neutralité".) In *François Suarez, sa philosophie et ses rapports avec sa thélogie* (1921), p. 522, Léon Mahieu admits that when Suarez "departs from the Angelic Doctor's way, it often happens that he does so along with some other more or less watered-down Thomist" and he cites in this regard Cajetan, Hervé, Victoria, Soto, Medina . . .; but he thinks he can say definitely that these authors "do not depart from Saint Thomas in anything but minor details", which is sometimes debatable.

[4] Cf. M.-Benoît Lavaud, O.P., "Le Père Garrigou-Lagrange", *Revue thomiste* 64 (1964): 184, note: "[Never] had he read Wolff, and he will never understand how Étienne

Gilson could say, and make people believe . . . that Father Garrigou-Lagrange owed his metaphysics to Wolff." Cf. É. Gilson, *Constantes*, 31–32 and 76–77. Albert Dondeyne, "Les problèmes philosophiques soulevés dans l'encyclique *Humani generis*", *Revue philosophique de Louvain* 49 (August 1951): 302. M. Blondel had written to the Rev. Wehrlé, July 11, 1904: "It was Wolff's dull dogmatism and the Philosophy of Lights that got Kant disgusted with the 'metaphysical illusion'; but he proved Aristotle's saying: Opposites are only varieties of the same thing" (*Lettres philosophiques* [Aubier, 1961], 233).

[5] See the long citation from Maurras (article in the *Revue catholique des idées et des faits*, March 28 and April 4, 1924 [Brussels]), in J. Maritain, *Une opinion sur Charles Maurras et le devoir des catholiques* (Plon, 1926), 14–16.

[6] Cf. H. de Lubac, "Augustinisme politique?", in *Théologies d'occasion* (DDB, 1984), 255–308.

[7] On Mandonnet's position: *Philosophe et théologie*, 103–106. It was Father Théry, O.P., Gilson says, "who finally opened my eyes".

[8] In 1950 he contributed to the *Mélanges Joseph Maréchal* (vol. I) a study on "Nature et portée des preuves scotistes de l'existence de Dieu".

[9] Cf. Louis de Rayemaeker, "L'Institut supérieur de philosophie de Louvain", in *Revue philosophique de Louvain* 49 (November 1951): 506–633. A significant fact: it was not the Catholic University of Louvain, but the Free University of Brussels, where Gilson, as an exchange professor from the Sorbonne, came in December 1923 to speak on Scholasticism.

[10] "The Christian teachers who . . . wished at that time to make themselves a philosophy free of any theological constraints, just rolled their idea of doctrine back into the past. . . . They constructed for themselves a medieval philosophy that was as independent of every theology as they wanted it

to be." Besides, they were naturally attracted by Thomistic tradition itself, as it had been presented for several centuries: "The Scholastics of the sixteenth century, all the way down to those of our own day, had a sort of dream: to construct, as a preamble to theology, a philosophy that owed nothing to theology except a kind of exterior control, a philosophy that, however, would agree perfectly with theology" (*Philosophe et théologie*, 102–103; *Introduction à la philosophie chrétienne*, 29).

[11] As early as 1922, in *Antimoderne*, 156: "Monsignor Deploige, in his *Conflit* . . . , shows what an original and *dominant* position Thomistic thought is taking today against the relative morality and 'behavioral science' formulated in the manner of Messrs. Durkheim and Lévy-Bruhl."

[12] Cf. *Introduction à la philosophie chrétienne*, 18: "There is no proof of the truth of this proposition 'God is', that could get us out of believing in the existence of the One whom we take at his word. The affirmation of God by faith is specifically something other than the affirmation of God by philosophical reasoning", etc.; *Philosophe et thélogie*, 87–88: "In 1931, Pastor A. Lecerf took the opportunity to denounce this doctrine that presented Catholic thought precisely as it ought to be presented so that a Protestant would have good reason to reject it"; this Calvinist theologian "believed in the essential difference between the natural order and the order of grace. This is why he held that natural theology, that is to say metaphysics, is 'incapable of forming the basis for *religious* knowledge', and by saying this, he . . . showed himself faithful to Catholic truth". It is evident from this example that Gilson did not participate in the discussions among "Thomists" just to be quibbling, nor solely for the purpose of establishing authentic doctrinal history.

[13] This was a *Traité élémentaire de philosophie a l'usage des classes*, 7th ed. (1921), edited by a group of professors from Louvain. Cf. *Philosophe et théologie*, 84–92.

[14]To Pegis, June 1, 1950: "This is what I'm getting ready to go and tell them in Rome." In the opening meeting of the Congress on the history of Scholasticism (Rome, September 6–10, 1950), Van Steenberghen, presenting a report on "L'interpretation de la pensée médiévale au cours du siècle écoulé", dodged any discussion with Gilson: "It remained for me to accomplish a delicate and complex maneuver: to describe the very important role played for more than thirty years by M. É. Gilson in the effort to interpret medieval thought. Fortunately fear of taking advantage of your kind attention gives me an excellent reason to excuse myself from this difficult job. M. Gilson has given a focus . . . to his predecessors' viewpoints that makes them more interesting while at the same time making them more vulnerable to attack" (*Revue philosophique de Louvain* 49 [1951]: 109–119). Van Steenberghen was always intractable in his opposition to Gilson. Cf. his important work on *La Philosophie au XIIIe siècle* (Louvain-Paris, 1966). On Bonaventure, Gilson's interpretation is "completely untenable", his definitions are "seriously wrong"; it is "unacceptable" to "present, under the trademark 'Saint Bonaventure's philosophy' or 'Saint Thomas' philosophy' a mutilated exposition of these authors' theology", it is an "inadmissible mutilation of these doctors' clearly-expressed thought". Like Renan, Gilson commits "a gigantic blunder" with regard to Averroës and "Latin Averroism": his opinion of Bacon comes from a "strange confusion, whose origin he alone can explain to us", etc. On Saint Thomas, "despite the good will and the talent of propagandists for 'Christian philosophy', their wild imaginings have often brought more confusion than enlightenment to ideas"; "the unsatisfactory methodology that M. Gilson wants to resurrect that consists in formulating metaphysical theses, not merely for the upbuilding of the Faith, but for use in theological problem-solving, . . . this is the world turned upside down. . . ." Van Steenberghen consoled himself by thinking

241

that due to the impact of more recent works, the "Gilsonian era was at an end" (pp. 208–209, 235, 264, 347, 366–367, 411, 424, 493, etc.).

[15] Cf. *Introduction à la philosophie chrétienne*, 110 ff., responding once again to the Christian philosophers who dreaded "seeing themselves credited with a bastard philosophy . . .": "Authentic Lutheranism on the one hand and philosophical rationalism on the other, have incessantly accused and still do not cease to accuse [Scholasticism] of having corrupted everything, of having corrupted the word of God by means of philosophy and by means of faith in a revelation that reason does not back up." See also L. 7, n. 1; Appendix II, n. 2. Cf. von Balthasar, *Gloire et Croix* 2:73: After Thomas Aquinas' *kairos* "an increasingly dualist world . . . will attempt, in both a Christian and a non-Christian manner, to separate philosophy from revealed theology, and to make an independent entity of each of them."

[16] In 1920 (January 26) Maritain gave a lecture-program at the Institut Supérieur de Philosophie in Louvain: "De quelques conditions de la renaissance thomiste", exalting "Thomist philosophy, that is, Scholastic philosophy in its pure form", as "a difficult discipline . . . , that requires a continually renewed reasoning effort", etc. (*Antimoderne* [1922], 121–167).

[17] In 1959, another invitation especially pleased Gilson: from the University of Freiburg im Breisgau, Germany, celebrating the fiftieth anniversary of its foundation: "The invitation came from the Faculty of Theology, and they are offering me an honorary doctorate in theology! *Tony! I shall feel very proud of this one!*" [Author's italics; Gilson had written this sentence in English—Tr.] [to Pegis, April 10, 1957). He regarded this honorary degree as the most meaningful he had received in his life, because it was in theology (Shook, *Gilson*, p. 334).

[18] "*Sharply disagreed on a number of essentials*" [Father L. K. Shook's original English—Tr.] (p. 346).

[19] *Distinguer pour unir* (1932), 256, note.

[20] He accused him of "an ambiguity that is not an instrument of philosophy"; ibid., 842; cf. pp. 843–835 and 839.

[21] Gilson, *Philosophe et théologie*, 58–59. "In rereading this fine book, after so many years" Maritain said he was struck by its "perceptiveness": "La possibilité de la philosophie chrétienne", *Revue des sciences religieuses*, 1958: 188, note. In his *Réflexions sur l'intelligence et sa vie propre* (Nouvelle Librairie nationale, 1924), 130, J. Maritain protested against a "peculiar philosophical process" employed by "certain neo-Thomists such as Father Rousselot".

[22] "Le thomisme et les philosophies existentielles", in *La Vie intellectuelle*, June 1945; Gilson gave Gabriel Marcel the lion's share of credit for separating the essentialist "Thomism" of the modern era from the mishmash of contemporary existentialisms. See, further, "Un philosophe singulier", in *Les Nouvelles littéraires*, June 19, 1958. Cf. Gabriel Marcel, Gaston Fessard, *Correspondance* (Beauchesne, 1985), annotation to Letter 84.

[23] *Maritain et son temps* (Grasset, 1959), 198.

[24] Maritain himself freely admitted the excesses he blamed on the militant enthusiasm of youth: "I would be more concerned now", he confessed, "that I've become too conciliatory"; but the reader will not find that to be very often the case. "I can think of some philosophies", Gilson said, "that can resist Jacques Maritain's thought . . . , but no philosophy can resist his presence"; except, he did not favor all philosophies with his presence. Cf. *Jacques Maritain, son oeuvre philosophique*, edited by the *Revue thomiste* (1930), xii and 3.

[25] To Pegis, December 7–8, 1959 (Shook, *Gilson*, 346).

[26] *Réflexions sur l'intelligence et sa vie propre*, 3rd ed., (1980), 129–130 (this passage will be cited by Bars, *Maritain et son temps*, 330–331).

[27] In *Distinguer pour unir* alone, one of Maritain's basic works, John of Saint Thomas is cited about fifty times; a

dozen times in *Science et sagesse*; ibid., 15 and 151: "The great commentators", "Cajetan and Saint Thomas teach . . .", etc. Cf. *Jacques Maritain, son oeuvre philosophique*, v–vi: his thought springs "from that of Saint Thomas and indeed from Saint Thomas' School"; a number of people consider him "too much of a 'Thomist', too fond of the "commentators'". This or that "adamantine thesis of Cajetan's", this or that "subtle, powerful page in John of Saint Thomas" bring his intellect an "incomparably bracing joyous feeling" (*Antimoderne* [1922], 158).

Cajetan was a "transitional figure"; he finds himself "in open intellectual and religious revolution. . . . He gives birth to tendencies and opinions that surprised many of his peers who were less free-spirited, or less up to date on current needs" (Mandonnet, in DTC 2:2). On these "current needs", that is to say the "general mental climate" at the time when Cajetan was compiling his great commentary on the *Summa* (the early years of the sixteenth century), I had a few words to say in *Surnaturel*, especially on p. 140. In the following century, John of Saint Thomas had good reason to write his fervent *Traité de la fidélité à saint Thomas* and could be called, also with good reason, a "second Saint Thomas"; the good reason being that his work depends no less entirely on the new perspective that, on the subject of man's final end, had caused both Saint Augustine and Saint Thomas to be thrown out simultaneously. See *Surnaturel*, part I, chapter 5, "Le système de la nature pure", and chapter 6, "Étapes de sa formation"; *Augustinisme et théologie moderne*, chapter 5, pp. 135–181: "Le thomisme conservateur au XVIe siècle". Whatever its merits, says Gilson in *Philosophe et théologie*, 108: "Scholasticism was never noted for its sense of history".

[28] H. Bars observed quite appropriately (*Maritain* [1959], 331) that Maritain, "who accepts the entire School and practices John of Saint Thomas, doesn't hesitate, either, to divorce himself from it—as indeed he recently did over the question

of the fall of the Angel Lucifer—on account of his ever-increasing fidelity to the spirit and to the letter of the Angelic Doctor's thought." On what Gilson called the "centrality" of the human problem, or the "centrality" of its "mystery", I did not, however (maybe this was an error on my part), find that he had ever gone all the way back to the authentic Saint Thomas.

[29] *Le Paysan de la Garonne* (DBB, 1966), 219.

[30] P. 201.

[31] Bars, *Maritain*, 331.

[32] *Distinguer pour unir*, chapter 7, "De la sagesse augustinienne", 579–611; *Science et sagesse*, 41–50; *Le Paysan de la Garonne*, 196.

[33] Cf. *Introduction*, 92–93, on a page from the *Confessions:* "If that isn't a real Christian philosophy and an authentic theology, there are no such things." See also Appendix II, n. 2.

[34] Thus, in *Le Docteur Angélique* (DDB, 1930), 29: "Each of his syllogisms is, as it were, a concretization of his prayers and tears, the kind of clear, calming grace his words bring to us doubtless comes from the fact that even his shortest text conceals invisibly the fertile seed of his desire, and the pure strength of his consuming love" (cited by Bars, *Maritain*, 106–107).

[35] *Antimoderne*, 32 and 147: cf. *Éléments de philosophie*, vol. I (1930); *Le Paysan de la Garonne*, 196–206; Raïssa Maritain, *Les Grandes Amitiés*, 466.

[36] Cf. Appendix III, L. 7, n. 4. *Philosophe et théologie*, 16–17; "The Apostles' Creed and the Catechism of the diocese of Paris have pervaded since my childhood all the key positions that govern my understanding of the world. . . . My philosophy today contains within itself the sum total of everything I believe"; ibid., 163–164: "For Aristotle's god to be included in the mainstream of Christian thought, he first would have had to stop being Aristotle's god, in order to become the

God of the Scriptures. Such a transmogrification goes a long way beyond what anyone, however liberal he might be when it comes to formulae, could call 'a few modifications'." Cf. chapters 4 and 5: "La théologie perdue" and "La théologie retrouvée". *Introduction à la philosophie chrétienne*, chapter 1: "Philosopher dans la foi"; chapter 10, p. 233: "The entire future of Christian philosophy depends on a long-awaited, desired, hoped-for restoration of the true notion of theology", etc. Our two philosophers successively turn away from each other and then join hands again; Maritain's quotations of Gilson reflect how anxious he is to agree with him, and that entails a certain vagueness in vocabulary.

[37] Title repeated in *Le Docteur angélique*, chapter 3, pp. 85–125. Cf. Shook, *Gilson*, 171.

[38] "Le thomisme et les philosophies existentielles", *La Vie intellectuelle* (1945); Shook, *Gilson*, 263; Maritain, *Le Docteur angélique*, 74.

[39] Cf. J.-H. Nicolas, O.P., in *Jacques Maritain, son oeuvre philosophique*, 218–235, with references; *Distinguer pour unir*, 153–158.

[40] In *Jacques Maritain, son oeuvre philosophique*, 3. Maritain will mention this word of Gilson's again in his *Court traité de l'existence*, in 1947: "I am not a neo-Thomist, all things considered I'd rather be a paleo-Thomist, but what I am, and hope to be, is just a Thomist" (pp. 9–10). But, on page 218, on Saint Thomas: "One of the main objects of his work was to distinguish irrefutably philosophy from theology, and thus to establish philosophy's autonomy." See p. 223 and n. 10, above.

[41] Cf. Shook, *Gilson*, 337–338.

[42] This fat volume of 660 pages reproduced the *Mellon Lectures in the Fine Arts* given in 1955. In 1958 Vrin printed *Peinture et Réalité, Problèmes et controverses*, which is not a French translation but "a companion piece to *Painting and Reality*".

[43] Letter of December 7, 1959 (Shook, *Gilson*, 346). Cf. in *Jacques Maritain, son oeuvre philosophique*, 123–141, the beautiful and devoted study by M. Thomas Calmel, O.P., "Frontières de la poésie", a study that is not, however, without a few reservations.

[44] Cf. his letter of December 18, 1983: "I'm about to touch another of poor Jacques' raw nerves . . ." (in Shook, *Gilson*, 362).

[45] *Philosophe et théologie*, 252.

[46] *Recherches et débats* 61 (December 1967): 240.